D0450261

BEYOND
POSSIBLE

ONE MAN, 14 PEAKS, and

the MOUNTAiNEERING

ACHiEVEMENT of a LiFETIME

YOUNG
READERS
EDITION

NIMSDAI PURJA

NATIONAL
GEOGRAPHIC

WASHINGTON, D.C.

Since 1888, the National Geographic Society has funded more than 14,000 research, conservation, education, and storytelling projects around the world. National Geographic Partners distributes a portion of the funds it receives from your purchase to National Geographic Society to support programs including the conservation of animals and their habitats. To learn more, visit natgeo .com/info.

For more information, visit national geographic.com, call 1-877-873-6846, or write to the following address:

National Geographic Partners, LLC
1145 17th Street NW
Washington, DC 20036-4688 U.S.A.

For librarians and teachers: nationalgeographic.com/books/ librarians-and-educators

More for kids from National Geographic: natgeokids.com

For rights or permissions inquiries, please contact National Geographic Books Subsidiary Rights: bookrights@natgeo.com

Designed by Amanda Larsen

Library of Congress Cataloging-in-Publication Data

Names: Purja, Nimsdai, author.
Title: Beyond possible / by Nimsdai Purja.
Description: Young readers' edition. | Washington, D.C. : National Geographic Kids, [2022] | Audience: Ages 10-14 | Audience: Grades 7-9 |
Identifiers: LCCN 2021029460 (print) | LCCN 2021029461 (ebook) | ISBN 9781426374050 (hardcover) | ISBN 9781426374555 (library binding) | ISBN 9781426374562 (ebook)
Subjects: LCSH: Purja, Nimsdai. | Great Britain. Royal Marines. Special Boat Service--Biography. | Mountaineers--Nepal--Biography. | Mountaineering--Himalaya Mountains Region. | Mountaineering--Karakoram Range.
Classification: LCC GV199.92.P86 A3 2022 (print) | LCC GV199.92.P86 (ebook) | DDC 796.522092 [B]--dc23
LC record available at https://lccn.loc .gov/2021029460
LC ebook record available at https:// lccn.loc.gov/2021029461

When Mount Everest is described in this book, the terms "tallest" and "highest" are both used. Although the words "tallest" and "highest" are commonly used interchangeably, they technically aren't the same terms. Mount Everest is the highest mountain on Earth with an elevation of 29,032 feet (8,849 meters) above sea level, but it isn't the tallest. The tallest mountain on Earth is Mauna Kea with a height of 32,696 feet (9,966 meters). Only 13,796 feet (4,205 meters) of this mountain is above sea level, so it isn't the highest mountain on Earth.

Printed in Canada
21/FC/1

To my mother, Purna Kumari Purja,
for working so hard to allow me to live my dreams,
and to the climbing community of Nepal,
home of the 8000ers.

Your extremes are my normality.

CONTENTS

KYRGYZSTAN

TAJIKISTAN

PAKISTAN

K2
28,251 ft (8,611 m)
July 24, 2019

Gasherbrum II
26,358 ft (8,034 m)
July 18, 2019

Gasherbrum I
26,509 ft (8,080 m)
July 15, 2019

Broad Peak
26,414 ft (8,051 m)
July 26, 2019

Nanga Parbat
26,657 ft (8,125 m)
July 3, 2019

C H I N A

Cho Oyu
(8,201 m) 26,906 ft
September 23, 2019

Mount Everest
29,032 ft (8,849 m)
May 22, 2019

Shishapangma
(8,027 m) 26,335 ft
October 29, 2019

Manaslu
(8,163 m) 26,782 ft
September 27, 2019

Dhaulagiri I
(8,167 m) 26,795 ft
May 12, 2019

NEPAL

Annapurna I
(8,091 m) 26,545 ft
April 23, 2019

Lhotse
(8,516 m) 27,940 ft
May 24, 2019

Makalu
(8,485 m) 27,838 ft
May 24, 2019

Kanchenjunga
(8,586 m) 28,169 ft
May 15, 2019

I N D I A

NORTH
AMERICA
EUROPE
ASIA
Pacific
Ocean
AFRICA
Area
Enlarged
Indian
Ocean
AUSTRALIA

MAP KEY

□ Phase 1
△ Phase 2
✚ Phase 3

Annapurna I Peak name
(8,091 m) 26,545 ft Elevation
April 23, 2019 Date summited

0 _____ 200 miles
0 _____ 200 kilometers

*Bay of
Bengal*

CHAPTER 1

A DANGEROUS FALL

T WAS JULY 3, 2019. THE WORLD SLIPPED OUT FROM beneath me as I skidded headfirst down the slushy, snowy side of Pakistan's Nanga Parbat. Everything seemed to rush by in a blur.

Only seconds earlier I'd felt secure, leaning hard into the steep slope and with solid footing. Then my grip slipped. The teeth of my crampons were unable to bite into the ice as I plummeted downward, slowly at first, then much quicker, building speed with every second. My brain was calculating the moments until I'd drop off the mountain forever.

If I died, there would be no one else to blame but myself. *I'd* chosen to climb the world's ninth highest mountain in brutal, whiteout conditions. *I'd* decided to climb all 14 "Death Zone" mountains in only seven months, knowing that each peak was higher than 26,000 feet (8,000 m), an altitude where the air has so little oxygen that the brain and body struggle to survive. And *I'd* chosen to let go of a fixed rope during my descent, a friendly gesture to allow another climber to pass as he nervously made his way down the mountain. Now I was out of control.

Was I scared of dying in those brief seconds? *No.* Testing my physical limits was exactly my hope in 2018, when I announced a plan to break the previous records for climbing Earth's 14 Death Zone peaks. The record had been set in 2013 by Kim Chang-ho, a Korean mountaineer. He finished the job in seven years, 10 months, and six days.

It was a wild idea, and aiming to shave away so much time from the record seemed absurd—perhaps beyond what was humanly possible. But I wanted to try. To do so, I quit the British military, where I served as a Gurkha soldier for several years before joining the Special Boat Service (SBS)—a wing of the special forces. Walking out on my career felt risky, but I believed in myself. I knew I could do it, even when others doubted me. I treated the challenge like a military mission. I'd even named my world-record-breaking attempt "Project Possible."

Though I had started high-altitude climbing only a few years earlier, I had become good at it. Once I started climbing into the Death Zone, I found it pretty easy to move quickly at great heights, taking 70 steps before pausing for a breath. Other mountaineers were only able to take four or five steps before pausing.

Another 100 feet (30 m) raced by on Nanga Parbat. As I fell, I knew I had to focus on my movement and increasing speed. Could I use my ice axe, digging it into the mountain to slow my fall? Yanking my ax underneath me, I held on to the head firmly, jamming the pick into the snow. But the snow was too soft—my axe wouldn't hold.

My confidence was fading when all of a sudden ... *there!* I spotted the fixed rope we were using to descend moments earlier.

If I could reach for it, I might be able to hang on. It was my last hope. I twisted, stuck out my arm, and made a grab for the cord ... *Got it!* Gripping with all my strength, my palm burning, I gradually pulled myself to a stop. *Was I OK?* Yes, though my legs shook with adrenaline and my heart banged against my chest.

> GRIPPING WITH ALL MY STRENGTH, MY PALM BURNING, I GRADUALLY PULLED MYSELF TO A STOP. *WAS I OK?*

Taking a second or two to reset, I rose to my feet and switched into a new rhythm, a more cautious stride.

To climbers on the line above, it may have looked as if I'd instantly regained control. But in reality, the fall had rattled me. My confidence had taken a hit. I gripped the rope tightly and double-checked each and every step until my confidence returned. As I planted my boots in the shifting snow, I told myself that death was going to come for me at some point—maybe on a mountain during Project Possible, maybe in old age decades from now—but not on Nanga Parbat. Not today.

Not today. But would I finish what I'd started?

CHAPTER 2

I HAVE HOPE

'D BEEN INSPIRED TO SCALE ALL 14 OF THE WORLD'S biggest peaks at record speed. I wanted to top Annapurna, Dhaulagiri, Everest, Kanchenjunga, Lhotse, Makalu, and Manaslu in Nepal; to race up Nanga Parbat, Gasherbrum I and II, K2, and Broad Peak in Pakistan; and finally, to conquer Tibet's Cho Oyu and Shishapangma mountains.

But why? These were some of the most extreme places on Earth. A challenge like that, with a deadline of only seven months, might have sounded crazy to most people. But to me, it was an opportunity to prove to the world that anything—*everything*—was possible if you put your heart and mind to it.

The adventure started with Mount Everest, located in the Himalaya in my homeland of Nepal. At 29,032 feet (8,849 m), it is the world's highest peak. When I was a kid, Everest felt like something distant and unreachable. My family was poor, and the trek from where we lived to Everest and back was not only expensive, it took about 12 days. So I never experienced it.

When I moved to England in 2003 as a Gurkha soldier serving with the British Armed Forces, people always asked the same question: "So what's Everest like?" Friends unfamiliar with Nepal's geography probably imagined that the mountain was just beyond my backyard. They looked unimpressed when I admitted that I'd never even seen the Everest Base Camp, let alone climbed above it. It even caused some other soldiers to question my strength.

"It's on your doorstep, mate, and you haven't bothered? And we thought Gurkhas were tough..."

After 10 years, the questioning and joking finally got to me. *OK*, I thought, *I'll start climbing.*

In December 2012, at the age of 29, I took my first steps toward the highest point on Earth and made the trek to the foot of Everest. Through a military friend, I'd been connected with the famous Nepali mountaineer Dorje Khatri, who offered to guide me to Base Camp. Dorje had scaled Everest several times and was a champion for the Sherpa guides. He defended their rights and campaigned for better pay. He was also a climate change activist and tried to alter the way everybody viewed the fragile ecosystem of the Himalaya. I couldn't think of a better person to go with on my first journey.

After making it to Base Camp, I decided that trekking wasn't enough. I wanted to go higher.

I convinced Dorje to teach me some of the skills I'd need to climb Everest. We traveled to the nearby peak Lobuche East, so I could begin learning. The work was slow but steady. Under Dorje's guidance, I pulled on a pair of crampons for the very first time and walked across a grass slope, feeling the bite of the crampons' steel points in the turf. The sensation was odd, but it gave me an idea of what I might experience during a proper mountain ascent. As we worked our way to the top, into the nipping cold and powerful winds, I felt the excitement of an expedition for the very first time.

On the summit, I was blown away by the view around me: The jagged Himalayan peaks were covered by a blanket of clouds, but here and there a peak poked through the gray mist. My adrenaline soared as Dorje pointed to Everest, Lhotse, and Makalu. A sense of pride washed over me, mixed with a feeling of anticipation. I'd already decided to climb those three peaks in the distance.

> AS WE WORKED OUR WAY TO THE TOP, INTO THE NIPPING COLD AND POWERFUL WINDS, I FELT THE EXCITEMENT OF AN EXPEDITION FOR THE VERY FIRST TIME.

As I sharpened my skills, my ambition grew. An advantage of being in the British military was that I had access to a variety of special courses. I joined one that taught soldiers the art of extreme cold-weather warfare and soon became a member of that unique group of mountain warfare specialists. Next, I climbed Denali, the highest peak in the United States. It is one of the Seven Summits, a group of the highest mountains on each continent: Denali (North America), Everest (Asia), Elbrus (Europe), Kilimanjaro (Africa), Vinson (Antarctica), Aconcagua (South America), and Carstensz Pyramid (Oceania).

At 20,310 feet (6,190 m), Denali was no joke. Isolated and brutally cold, the temperatures there sometimes dropped to minus 58°F (-50°C), which presented a serious problem for a novice climber like me. But Denali was also a perfect training ground. I learned rope skills and put my Special Forces endurance training to good use, dragging my sled through the thick snow for hours on end, taking care not to fall into one of the many crevasses on the mountain.

Then in 2014, I climbed Dhaulagiri, my first peak in the Death Zone. Dhaulagiri, part of the Himalayan mountain range, was a beast. Nicknamed the White Mountain because of the deep powder coating its steep and intimidating slopes, it was regarded as one of the most dangerous climbs in the world.

Dhaulagiri's biggest danger was avalanches, which swept away everybody and everything in their path. In 1969, five Americans and two Sherpas were swiped from the mountain. Six years later, six members of a Japanese expedition were killed when a wall of snow buried them alive. Dhaulagiri wasn't an adventure to be taken lightly, especially for a climber like me with only 18 months of experience and limited knowledge of the difficult conditions on extreme peaks. But eager to improve my climbing skills, I decided I was going up as soon as I was given leave from fighting with the Gurkhas in Afghanistan. A close friend from the British Special Forces went with me on the trip. (To protect his privacy, I will call him James.)

Our arrival at Base Camp was poorly timed. We were joining up with a larger expedition that had been getting used to, or acclimatizing to, the thin air for a month. An avalanche had prevented their trip to Everest, so they decided to climb Dhaulagiri instead.

James and I were behind schedule because of our limited leave from the military. We didn't have the same amount of time to acclimate to the high altitude as the other mountaineers did, and James was really struggling. It took us three days longer than the others to complete the journey.

Later, a fellow climber asked us, "What do you guys do?" He'd noticed that we didn't seem like seasoned climbers, and I knew what he was thinking—were we inexperienced, crazy guys who should be avoided when it came time to make the difficult push to the summit.

There was no way James or I was about to reveal our full military roles. We were bound to certain levels of secrecy. Also, both of us liked the idea of being judged on our mountaineering skills rather than our combat expertise.

"Oh, we're in the military," I said eventually, hoping for an end to the questions.

The climber raised an eyebrow quizzically. Our expedition mates wrote us off as clueless tourists, but that didn't bother us. At Base Camp we prepared enthusiastically for our climb. In order to slowly acclimate to the altitude as we climbed, our plan for the next week was to climb daily to Camps 1 and 2, the first of four tent camps along the route to the peak. We'd then sleep lower down the mountain, until we felt ready for our summit push.

When we began our first acclimatization ascent, James was still struggling. This had first become clear on our Base Camp trek, but once we started the serious business of climbing to Camp 1, he was unable to maintain the pace as I pushed ahead. Altitude sickness was really hurting him.

As I climbed onward the next day, James fell behind again. Before too long, I'd also tired myself out. In a rush of excitement, I'd wanted to show off my speed, but I pushed too far ahead. As I rested at Camp 1 for a couple of hours, brewing a cup of hot tea and waiting for our group to arrive, a horrible thought struck me. *Was James still alive?*

As well as regularly trembling with avalanches, Dhaulagiri was known for its deep crevasses. There was every chance James and his Sherpa might have tumbled into one. If that were the case, it was unlikely they'd be discovered for days, if at all. In a slight panic, I packed up my pot and cup and headed down toward Base Camp to find them.

It didn't take long. Two people were moving slowly below me. I soon realized it was my climbing party, but James was in a worse state than before.

I reached out to lighten his load, but James seemed hesitant. He didn't want to give in to the pain, but I insisted. When fighting through war zones with the Special Forces, an attitude of that kind would have been considered commendable. On a mountain as dangerous as Dhaulagiri, it was far more risky.

I said to James, "If you want to get to the summit, let me help you."

James gave in. Slowly but steadily, we worked our way back up to Camp 1, but the effort had taken its toll on me, too. I'd done too much, and the mountains were delivering their first major lesson: Never burn yourself out unnecessarily. From then on, I promised not to waste vital energy; I would work hard only when I needed to. When the time arrived a few days later to make my first ever summit push, I made sure to hang at the back of the group as we snaked our way to the peak of Dhaulagiri. This was partly out of respect for the Sherpas leading us to the top, but also because I'd never climbed such a huge mountain before and I didn't want to experience another energy slump.

That's when I noticed the ever changing work of the Sherpa guides within an expedition party. Every now and then, the leading Sherpa would take a break from plowing a path with his body through the waist-high snowdrifts, allowing one of his teammates to take over for a while. He would then fall to the back of the line until it was his turn to head the charge once more, while the rest of us matched his footprints in the snow. This was a technique known as trailblazing. The lead Sherpa was helping the expedition party to follow a much smoother route upward.

Suddenly, a climber in front of me stepped out of the line and started his way to the front of the pack to help.

I shouted up at him. "Hey, bro! What are you doing? The Sherpas aren't going to get upset, are they?"

He waved me away. "No man, I'm doing my bit, helping the Sherpa brothers."

I'd assumed that leading the group in such a way was disrespectful to the expedition guides. It turned out I was wrong. One of the Sherpas soon explained it to me.

"Nims, the snow is so deep. If you have the energy and can help out up front too, please do."

Encouraged, I soon took the lead and drove forward. My legs lifted and pushed as I raised my feet out of the snow. My thighs and calves ached with the endeavor, but my lungs were light. The fatigue that hindered other climbers at such a high altitude didn't seem to bother me. I was strong. *Boom! Boom! Boom!* Every step arrived with power. When I turned back to see how far I'd come, I was shocked to notice the rest of my climbing party. They were little black dots below.

Careful not to overdo it like I did before, I worked my way slowly to the next ridgeline, waiting an hour until the remainder of the group caught up. When they later gathered around me, the lead Sherpa guide shouted excitedly and slapped me on the back. Other climbers who had looked down on me a few days earlier were now shaking my hand.

By the time I reached the peak, I had trailblazed more than 70 percent of the route. I was not only surprised at what I'd achieved, I was inspired by my high-altitude abilities.

WHEN I WAS A KID, BECOMING A MOUNTAIN CLIMBER wasn't something I had in mind. I wanted to be one of two things. The first was to serve as a Gurkha soldier, like my dad. Gurkhas are respected as a fearless military force. They have fought in many wars throughout history, including in World War II, and later, in wars in Iraq and Afghanistan.

My second career ambition was to be a government official. I wanted to help the poor. Even as a kid, I understood that the people around me had very little and that the poverty rates were incredibly high in Nepal. I wanted to do something about that.

Born in a village called Dana in western Nepal, I was poor from the beginning. There was a gap of around 18 years between me and my older brothers, Ganga, Jit, and Kamal, and three years between me and my younger sister, Anita. We didn't have any money, but we were a loving family, and I was a happy kid.

Although Dad was serving with the Indian Gurkha regiment, his salary alone wasn't enough to support the family. So Mom started working on the village farm for money. Most of the time, at least one of the kids was strapped to her back in a cloth. The workload of caring for a young family while bringing money home through hard labor must have been exhausting, but she didn't quit. A lot of my work ethic came from my mother. She was a huge influence on me.

Mom had not been educated, which must have annoyed her. But she didn't let that stop her from achieving great things. She had a vision for how to help other women in the area and eventually become an activist in Nepal. Mom worked to support education for women, and she fought for what she believed in. Most weeks she earned barely enough to put food on the table, but the family survived. Once my brothers were old enough, they were put to work, too. It was their job to wake up at 5 a.m. and walk for two hours to find and cut grass for the family's three buffalo. Then they walked to school.

I had it a little easier. Our garden had several orange trees, and once the fruit ripened in the fall, I'd climb into the branches and shake the limbs until they were empty. The ground was soon covered in fruit, and I'd eat my way through it until I was full.

When I was four years old, my family moved to the jungle village of Ramnagar, in the town of Chitwan, 227 miles (365 km) away from Dana. My parents had been worried about landslides threatening Dana, where several fast-flowing rivers had a tendency to flood.

With the jungle at our doorstep, Mom would go into the undergrowth to grab wood for the fire. I spent my time exploring our new home. Most of the time I headed for the nearby river, hanging out on the banks and hunting for crabs and prawns. I was happiest in nature; adventure seemed to be everywhere.

Life soon improved. When my brothers, who were much older than me, went off to join the Gurkhas, they said they hoped to help me have a better life. Every month, part of their pay was sent home, a gift to fund my education at Small Heaven Higher

Secondary, a boarding school in Chitwan where classes were taught in English. This was a luxury, and Mom often mentioned that it was temporary.

"One day they are going to be married," she would say of my brothers. "They'll have families of their own to look after, and they won't be able to support your education anymore."

But even as a young kid, I already had a plan in mind to support the family. "Look, it's fine," I told Mom. "I'll become a teacher. Then I'll be able to look after *you*." But really I wanted to be a Gurkha.

CHAPTER 3

FINDING STRENGTH

AROUND AGE 10, I CAUGHT TUBERCULOSIS, A SERIOUS and common disease in Nepal. I fought it off. Years later, I was diagnosed with asthma. When the doctor explained its long-term impacts, I thought, *Yeah, no problem.* It was not going to stop me from living a full life, and it didn't. Even with asthma, I ran through the woods and over long distances in school races for fun.

From an early age, I also believed in the power of positive thinking; I didn't allow illnesses to get in my way. I trusted myself to heal. *I believed.* That same attitude eventually steered me into the British military, where I fulfilled my dream of becoming a Gurkha.

The selection process to get into the Gurkha regiment was tough. Every applicant between the ages of 17 and 21 went through a thorough physical and mental assessment. For example, anyone with more than four tooth fillings was rejected. Grades in school were equally as important.

I was one of only 18 applicants to pass the physical tests, but on the overall scoring, I ranked 26th. Only 25 individuals were accepted into the Gurkha Selection each year. Angry and disappointed, I considered giving up on my dream of joining the regiment. In the end, I moved past those feelings. I knew I had it in me to join the bravest military force in the world. I repeated the rigorous training process. A year later, in 2002, I was successful. After that, I was accepted as part of the British Army and would later become a member of the Queen's Gurkha Engineers. Within two weeks of being selected, I flew to England where I joined the Gurkha Training Company. I had never been abroad, let alone as far away as England.

WHEN OUR PLANE LANDED AT LONDON'S HEATHROW Airport in January 2003, I was shocked. It was cold. We traveled the highway heading to the north of the country. The route was full of sheep, hills, and the occasional service station. It wasn't what I had expected, and my confidence at settling into the local culture fell.

First, the weather was awful, and the wind and rain were really strong. It always seemed to be coming down sideways. Also, the language barrier posed a big problem. Even though my written English had been pretty good at school, I was absolutely lost when it came to accents. It all sounded alien to me. The very first person I met in England was from Liverpool. When I shook his hand to say hello, I had no idea what he was saying back to me.

In Nepal I'd been educated only by reading, listening, and talking. Nobody warned me about different regional dialects. When I was thrown into real-life situations with British people,

I was at a serious disadvantage. In the first few weeks, I often drifted through conversations thinking, *What?*

But when it came to the business of fighting, I was more than ready. I went through a 36-week Gurkha training course. Once I passed the recruit training, I joined the Gurkha Engineers. I was then instructed to choose a skill to learn from a list that included carpentry and plumbing. I opted to work in building and structural finishing. For nine months I learned how to plaster walls, paint, and decorate. The effort was worthwhile. I knew that if a military career didn't work out for me, I'd have a profession to fall back on.

Later, I learned all the skills required of a combat engineer and started on a series of field exercises. In 2007, after completing a 13-week commando training course, I was deployed to Afghanistan. There, I helped locals build a new government—a big challenge.

For the most part I was assigned to work with the Royal Marines Commandos. They were super-soldiers, but they were humble, too, which I appreciated.

At times I'd hear stories about operations that were going on away from where we were: hostage rescues, arrests of Taliban members, and door-kicking raids, all of them performed by the SAS (Special Air Service) or SBS (Special Boat Service). As far as I was concerned, their work represented a step up, even from the Gurkhas. I wanted to be one of those guys.

AS FAR AS I WAS CONCERNED, THEIR WORK REPRESENTED A STEP UP, EVEN FROM THE GURKHAS. I WANTED TO BE ONE OF THOSE GUYS.

Toward the end of 2008, I sized up my options and decided to sign up to join the SBS.

An intense six-month test determined which soldiers had the stamina and strength to join this special force. I was accepted in 2008. After six years with the Gurkhas, I was moving on. My moment to join the military elite had arrived.

CHAPTER 4

PURSUING EXCELLENCE

NOBODY BELIEVED ME WHEN I SAID MY MISSION WAS to join the Special Boat Service, probably because no Gurkha had made it into its ranks before. As a member of the SBS, every operator in the squadron had to be able to swim and dive during combat. Gurkhas come from a land-locked country, so the odds seemed stacked against me. But I understood that to become a Special Forces operator, it was important to adapt. I worked hard to fit in with the other soldiers and to prepare physically. I put myself through intense training.

Combat swimming would play a major role in my training, but I wasn't the greatest swimmer. So, I swam laps in the pool for as many miles as my body could handle. I rarely made it to bed before midnight. I'd collapse, exhausted, sometimes getting up again at 2 a.m. to train some more.

On weekends, I worked on my running. Every morning, I jogged for hours. I'd rise at 8 a.m. with two or three Gurkha buddies to practice. We ran using a relay system in which one soldier—me—was prevented from taking a break. One soldier went with me for six miles (10 km), pushing me to keep up with his strong pace. Once he ran his distance, another running partner took over, and we'd complete another six miles. This work was draining, but I never considered giving up.

I understood that when fighting with the Special Forces, there would be no time to rest, so training as hard as I could seemed the best way forward. I fought against doubt. My teammates and senior officers in the Gurkhas assumed that elite military service was beyond me. None of them grasped how dedicated I'd become, or how my mindset would help me to achieve impossible feats in the years ahead. I had hope. *And hope was everything.*

NONE OF THEM GRASPED HOW DEDICATED I'D BECOME, OR HOW MY MINDSET WOULD HELP ME TO ACHIEVE IMPOSSIBLE FEATS IN THE YEARS AHEAD.

When I finally made it to the selection process in 2009, every day our group faced an incredible test of physical and emotional strength. Held over six months, the process began with the Hills Phase, and included a series of timed runs over the Brecon Beacons mountain range in South Wales, U.K. To deal with the pressure, I focused only on the 24 hours ahead, rather than worrying about the tests lined up for my group over the coming weeks.

Because of the color of my skin, I found it impossible to blend in or to hide in the middle of the group with the other guys. Though everybody screwed up from time to time, my mistakes were usually spotted immediately and often from a distance. The yelling and jeering would start shortly after, but I was able to maintain my concentration. During one test march, I failed the course's time requirement by barely a minute.

Immediately I felt the pressure. Every day, the tests became harder. After failing one, I knew the following 24 hours would become even more demanding.

The next morning was set to be a beast, too: The final day of the Hills Phase was a speed march over almost 19 miles (30 km) of terrain. This was followed by the infamous final march, a test of endurance over more than 37 miles (60 km). We each had to carry about 80 pounds (36 kg) of gear. And the march had to be done in under 20 hours.

Either do this, Nims, or go home, I thought the following morning.

Mentally and physically, I was finding it within my grasp to adapt to the toughest challenges the Hills Phase could drop on me. I felt strong, and, after nearly a full day of exertion, I crossed the finish line. I was the fastest recruit of the day.

In the face of my toughest challenge yet, I hadn't cracked. I'd bent and flexed. I was strong.

I passed additional specialist courses, and was confirmed as a member of the SBS.

Another dream was coming true.

ALMOST AS SOON AS I WAS CONFIRMED, THE WORK began. One minute I was training in a boat, the next I was throwing myself out of a plane. Suspended by my parachute, I floated through the air above the sea below. My life was fast-paced, demanding, and never dull.

Once in the SBS, each operator undertakes one of several roles to become even more prepared for a particular job. I opted to become a trauma medic. It was my responsibility to patch up any wounds or injuries sustained by my teammates.

Finally, I was thrust into action for real in July 2010, when I fought in a series of war zones. During my work with the Special Forces, I became a seasoned soldier. I was able to stay calm under extreme pressure because of my training and experience, but also because the Gurkha spirit kept me motivated during tough times. I had a code: bravery over everything else. There was no other way for me to live.

CHAPTER 5

ON TOP OF
THE WORLD

WHEN I WAS AT WAR FOR PROLONGED PERIODS OF
time, life became even harder. But I didn't crumble.
During Gurkha Selection, I hadn't wanted the
Directing Staff to think I was unable to cope when
operating at the edges of my limits. During war, I certainly didn't
want the enemy to sense that I'd become weak, tired, or scared.
By focusing intensely on the job at hand, I disguised my pain and
suffering. This focus helped to shut out the chaos around me.

Another way I dealt with the intensity of my job was by taking advantage of the opportunities in the military's highly special-
ized climbing courses. I scaled challenging peaks and descended
sheer rock faces. I wanted to earn a place on the upcoming 2015
G200E climb of Everest, an expedition of a team of Gurkha soldiers. Once my spot was secured, I was required to train a number of recruits from the Gurkha regiment who were hopefuls
looking to join the same expedition. Together we climbed more
than 20,000 feet (6,100 m) of Makalu, the fifth largest mountain
in the world. Makalu was chosen because it was the perfect

mountain to experience the same altitudes as Everest. Also, dealing with the challenges on Makalu gave us practice in the technical climbing essential for making it up Everest.

After that expedition, I decided to take on Ama Dablam, the mountain I'd fallen in love with during that trek with my friend and climbing mentor Dorje in 2012. Now, in 2014, I took an unusual route up, climbing a near-vertical section of the mountain and going from Base Camp to Camp 2, rather than resting and acclimating to the altitude at Camp 1. My efforts paid off. I reached the top of one of the Himalaya's trickiest mountains in around 23 hours, and it felt great.

But soon after, I was struck by a double whammy of tragedies. The first was news that Dorje had been killed in an avalanche on Everest on April 18, 2014. This hit me hard. Everest was closed for the rest of the season after guides refused to work as a mark of respect for the deceased.

Several months later, it was announced that my military squadron would be rotated into action in May 2015. This was the same time the 2015 G200E trip was scheduled. As a result, I lost my spot on the climbing team. I was more than disappointed. A lot of what I'd been working on had been leading me toward that one expedition. By scaling Dhaulagiri, Ama Dablam, and Denali, my body and mind felt ready, but I had to get over my disappointment. It wasn't my job to be a professional mountaineer. My role was to operate in war—not to sulk. Looking back at it, though, maybe fate figured into my being taken out of the climbing team.

When the 2015 Gurkha expedition members were at Everest Base Camp, a large earthquake caused a huge avalanche. It was worse than the 2014 avalanche that took my friend Dorje.

Luckily, nobody from the expedition team was seriously injured. I learned that the G200E, along with every expedition that year, was being canceled. A new date was set for May 2017, and I hoped to make it back on the team by then.

I made sure to improve my climbing skills, so that if 2017 went according to plan, I'd be ready for Everest. But then, unexpectedly, an opportunity to climb the world's tallest mountain emerged in the spring of 2016. My military deployment plans were changed at the very last minute. I had spent the early part of the year training for one top secret combat mission, but I was suddenly asked to operate in another. I didn't want to do it, but I had no choice. Luckily, a happy twist was coming.

"Look, Nims, we'll give you four weeks' leave instead of the standard three," said my sergeant major. "How does that sound?"

It sounded good to me, as I saw an opportunity.

Maybe I could climb Everest?

Logistically it was a long shot, and the expedition came loaded with risk. Because of time constraints, I wouldn't have the luxury of a two-month period to acclimate to the altitude, as most people do when climbing the highest peaks. Financially, the odds were stacked against me, too. It was very expensive to climb Everest. But realizing the opportunity might never present itself again, I knew I needed to make it happen. I took out all of my savings, and managed to get a bank loan. I booked a flight from England to Nepal's capital, Kathmandu.

When I left England, I figured that most people climbing Everest that season were already moving toward Camp 3 and preparing to push for the summit. I knew with a Sherpa's support I'd be able to make the trek to Base Camp and then move to the higher camps with ease. But I didn't want the support of a Sherpa.

I wanted to climb Everest solo.

It was a crazy idea and I knew it, especially as I'd only been climbing the big mountains for a couple of years. But I was confident that my extensive military climbing training and the expeditions to Dhaulagiri, Ama Dablam, and Makalu had given me what I needed: enough knowledge, and the physical and mental strength to survive.

My mission was in place. I was taking on the world's tallest peak.

WITH A RAPIDLY NARROWING SUMMIT WINDOW AT THE end of May, the majority of people I'd encountered on my way to Everest didn't expect me to make it to the top in just three weeks, especially since I was going solo.

I shrugged it all off. I was focused. My plan for making it to the summit in such a limited window was to do everything quicker than was recommended without wasting too much energy. I trekked to Base Camp at speed, making it to the foot of Everest in only three days. Rather than heading to Camp 1, I headed straight for Camp 2 at 21,000 feet (6,400 m). This trip usually took most people a month, or longer, as they settled into the high altitudes. I was foregoing the luxury of time and rest, trying to adapt and survive. But I quickly paid a heavy price for my impatience.

Having passed Camp 1, but still far from Camp 2, I became exhausted. I wasn't acclimated to the altitude, and my heavy back pack was taking its toll. I was also severely dehydrated. Every step in my crampons along the icy climb felt like a monumental effort.

The sun was high. At times I felt like I was melting under its heat. Sweat burned my eyes and I could barely see. There were dangers everywhere.

I was heading through an area marked with crevasses. Though I was clipped onto a safety rope, I knew that if the ground were to give way beneath me, or if I were to slip from one of the ladders used to bridge icy ridges, it might be days before I was discovered. I was close to my breaking point with all of the physical and emotional effort. My eyes brimmed with tears. For the first time in years, self-doubt was getting to me.

I'm not strong enough to make it to Camp 2. But I really don't want to go back to Camp 1 either.

> **I WAS CLOSE TO MY BREAKING POINT WITH ALL OF THE PHYSICAL AND EMOTIONAL EFFORT.**

I had to refocus. Whenever I'd been in life-or-death situations in the past, I thought of my wife, Suchi. Thinking of her restored my focus and determination.

Let's do this.

I attempted to reboot. After sucking in a few deep breaths, my heart felt full again. My pep talk jolted me back to life, and I found an extra reserve of strength. I pressed on to Camp 2.

Boom! Boom! Boom! Every step felt like an achievement. *Boom! Boom! Boom!* Every step was a positive push ahead.

As I'd discovered on Dhaulagiri, it was fairly easy to burn out at high altitudes, but I hadn't yet experienced the full medical consequences when making that kind of mistake firsthand. That moment was soon to arrive.

By the time I'd set up my tent at Camp 2, I was feeling good again. I ate some lunch and hung out with a couple of Sherpa friends before pushing up another 500 feet (150 m) and back, in order to acclimate. My hope was to avoid the pounding headaches that sometimes dogged me when sleeping at high altitude. But I took it too far. By the time I lay down in the tent to rest, my lungs were aching. I was developing high-altitude pulmonary edema (HAPE), which meant fluid was accumulating in my lungs. Without treatment I might die. I had to recover.

As I rested in my sleeping bag, listening to the wheeze of my straining lungs, I felt frustrated. That extra push had broken me. Now every breath took so much effort.

Nims, you should have known. You're a mountaineer and a medic! You have all the knowledge in the world about altitude sickness. Why couldn't you have been more careful?

I'd been wrong to test my limits this way despite my military training and experience on other mountains. This was Everest. The line between good and bad decisions was even narrower in mountaineering than in war, because the extremes of life were so dramatic on the world's highest peaks. After only 24 hours on Everest, I returned to Base Camp for a medical check and a period of recovery. I spent the time rethinking my summit push. There was no way I was going to allow Everest to defeat me. But as it turned out, I would have to wait.

I visited with two doctors at Base Camp, and both told me not to go back up in my condition. I didn't take their word for it.

A doctor friend of mine was also working somewhere on Base Camp. I tracked him down, hoping for a different diagnosis, one that would allow me to return to climbing. Instead, I was given the third and final warning of the day.

"Nims, man, you've got to get off the mountain. That's a pulmonary edema. You can't mess around."

I was going to have to take my recuperation a little more seriously after all. I traveled back by helicopter to the town of Lukla, which has a small airport. I got x-rays and had some downtime for a few days. At that point I knew that if I was to scale Everest, I'd have to ascend with more caution. This didn't fill me with confidence, because my leave days from the military were flying by, and the climbing season was drawing to a close.

Still, I was determined not to let this physical challenge derail my plans. As I recovered, I filled my head with positive thoughts. I told myself I'd make it to the top, no problem. I focused on success. But there was another realization I had to deal with: I knew I couldn't summit Everest alone. I needed a Sherpa to help me. However, there was no way I was taking an easy ride to the top. I wanted to employ the least experienced guy I could find, because I still hoped for a serious challenge. In addition, Nepali Sherpas were underappreciated and underpaid. Climbers scaling Everest traveled light. Meanwhile, their Sherpas and porters lugged heavy loads of rope, food, and other necessities. They received very little pay for their efforts and next to no credit. However, once an inexperienced Sherpa had climbed Everest, he could raise his fees. I wanted to give somebody that opportunity. A Sherpa could also help me down the mountain if I developed the same lung condition again.

Back at Everest Base Camp, I met Pasang Sherpa. He was a young porter with zero experience of making it to Everest's peak. He would be the perfect person for my adventure. Pasang was so unprepared that he owned only an old summit suit and a beaten-up pair of boots.

"This is great, Nims," he said, pulling on the thermal layers, gloves, and other clothing I'd given him. "If I can get you to the top, I'll be able to charge three times as much for my services."

Knowing the trip would change both our lives forever, we started our climb. *All we could do was hope for the best.*

PASANG AND I MOVED STEADILY UP THE MOUNTAIN. THE wind had picked up; conditions were harsh, but our two-man team was able to press ahead from Camp 2 to 3, pitching a tent and sleeping as the weather became worse. My lungs felt good; I was holding up physically. But when we eventually pushed for the summit later that night, I made sure to watch the expedition ahead. I wanted to be sure we were not moving up blindly through the dark, especially during my first ever summit push on Everest. I'd already had one brush with death, and I didn't want to experience another.

With the peak in sight, we pulled ourselves along the fixed line that tethered us to the mountain. By 4 a.m. we had made it past the famous Hillary Step, a tricky and tall boulder face that every climber on this route has to get past if they are to reach the world's highest point. (In the 2015 earthquake, the Hillary Step was altered when its largest boulder fell away, but people still refer to it as a landmark.) A rush of excitement pulsed through me. *I was going to do it!*

Our timing to the summit had been perfect: The sun was about to appear over the Himalaya. We had made it! I treasured the excitement, but Pasang seemed edgy. The strong winds had intensified, and we were both becoming a little unsteady on our feet.

"Nims, we have to go back," he said.

"But we've just got here!"

"Yeah, but this is a dangerous time. People die on the way down because they wait too long and get caught by the weather."

Despite Pasang's lack of experience on Everest, I knew he was right. The winds were also known to reach almost 100 miles an hour (160 km/h) at the peak from time to time. The most important part of any climb was to get back down, quickly and safely. But I just couldn't leave so soon.

I checked my oxygen levels. I was in fairly good shape, and according to my watch there was plenty of time for a safe descent. I told myself that Pasang was probably panicking because he was new to the mountain. Turning around for Base Camp was his priority now.

"Listen, brother, I risked everything to be here, and I'm feeling strong," I said. "So, I'm not going down until I see the sun rising."

"No, Nims. *No, no, no!*"

"I can make it down, no problem," I told Pasang firmly, giving him permission to leave.

He turned away sadly, but I was happy to wait alone. As I watched him trudge down the mountain, the sun climbed higher above the Himalaya, melting over the snowcapped peaks in a wash of orange and pink. It seemed to burn away the wispy clouds below. Himalayan prayer flags fluttered behind me. At that moment, I was the only person on Earth at its highest point. I took off my goggles to feel the cold air against my eyes. The view was every bit as spectacular as I'd imagined. Waiting for the morning light had been the right decision. But I wasn't going to stay around for much longer.

I took one last look at the epic views around me and trudged down, visualizing a celebration at Base Camp. Days earlier, I had been bedridden with sore lungs, yet I'd still been able to climb the world's tallest mountain. My self-confidence grew.

ON MY WAY DOWN, I SAW AN ABANDONED CLIMBER ON the terrain below. I approached the person to help.

At first, I wasn't sure if the mountaineer was alive. Leaning in close, I immediately checked for any vital signs. It was a woman and she was seemingly pinned to the spot, unable to move. Her goggles were gone, and when I looked around in the snow there was no sign of them anywhere. Physically, she was in bad shape. She was semiconscious and barely able to speak. Finding her pulse was a struggle. I guessed she wasn't going to make it down unless somebody moved her quickly.

Luckily, I was still feeling fairly strong. I had to get her to Camp 4, where she'd hopefully receive the help she so badly needed. But time was against us, and if I couldn't find her a pair of goggles before the sun had risen fully, the woman might suffer snow blindness, a painful burn to the retinas from UV rays at high altitude. It was like having sand rubbed into your eyes. I cranked up the oxygen in her tank and tried to wake her.

"Hey, you're going to be okay," I shouted, shaking her gently. "What's your name?"

I heard a mumble. She was talking. I leaned in closer.

"Seema ..."

Seema! That was something to work with. If I could keep her talking, there was a fighting chance I'd save her life.

"Where are you from?"

"India," she whispered.

"Okay, Seema, I'm going to get you home."

She seemed to nod. I heard her mumbling again, but I couldn't tell if she was showing signs of delirium or if she was trying to tell me something. I radioed down to Camp 4, where I knew a rescue team was resting. I hoped Seema's condition could be dealt with at Camp 4 because the air would be a little thicker at least. The team there would have oxygen, too.

"Guys, it's Nims," I said. "There's a woman, Seema, stuck here. Can you help her?"

A voice responded right away. "Last night we rescued a climber all the way from the South Summit, and now we're in bad shape. Can you bring her down to Camp 4 yourself? We can help her from here. If we come up again, one or two of us might die."

"Sure, no problem," I said, even though I knew that helping her get down could become a big problem.

Pulling a length of old rope dangling from one of the fixed lines on the mountain, I wound it around Seema's waist, securing it tight. I then heaved, edging her slowly down toward Camp 4, which was more than 1,400 feet (427 m) below. With every pull, Seema moaned in pain.

After about an hour, and, having been dragged for 656 feet (200 m) lower, Seema seemed capable of standing. I pulled her up and encouraged her to attempt a few steps, and then a few more, until gradually we started making progress. But the effort was painful.

Finally, with about 82 feet (25 m) to go, I realized that Seema didn't have it in her to continue. She was too weak. I was hurting, too, barely able to stand. My climb through the night had finally caught up with me, and the adrenaline of scaling Everest had worn off. I fell to my knees and radioed for help. A team of

Sherpas rushed from a nearby tent and dragged us both to safety. Once sheltered from the freezing winds, I summoned enough strength to call Base Camp.

"Guys, this is Nims. I'm at Camp 4 with Seema. She's in bad shape, but the rescue team is looking after her now."

There was a crackle on the other end of the line. One of Seema's expedition buddies was shouting excitedly. In the background, I heard other voices as people gathered around the radio.

"Nims, that's amazing! Thank you."

There was a pause. "Are *you* okay?"

I found myself at the tipping point. My oxygen was close to running out, and if I hung around for too long, there was every chance I might die. Knowing that Seema had enough in her own tank and that rescuers were with her, I realized my work was done.

MY OXYGEN WAS CLOSE TO RUNNING OUT, AND IF I HUNG AROUND FOR TOO LONG, THERE WAS EVERY CHANCE I MIGHT DIE.

"Guys, if I stay here any longer, you may have to rescue me as well. I'm going down now."

Hours later, I staggered into Base Camp and collapsed, instantly falling asleep in my tent. I woke the next day to good news: Seema was alive, and she had been successfully taken off the mountain.

In the aftermath of Seema's solo rescue, I'd learned a serious lesson: By using oxygen during my expedition, it had been possible to save her. Without it, the chances of me summoning up enough energy to conduct a rescue would have been slim to none. For that reason, from now on, I would always climb above the higher camps with bottled air.

My accomplishment summiting Everest made me the first serving Gurkha to have scaled the world's tallest mountain. Had that detail been publicized in a newspaper report, there's every chance the G200E would have been scrapped. Why? Because the goal of the G200E was to get the first serving Gurkhas to the top of Everest. I was a Gurkha, and I had already done it. I needed anonymity to make sure the rescheduled G200E could take place. When I returned home, my family and close friends were sworn to secrecy.

Every morning for a week, I scanned the newspapers for any news of my rescue efforts on Everest. I had requested that it be kept private, as it could have affected my position in the military. But from what I could tell, nothing had been written—at least, nothing that mentioned me by name. Shortly after returning from Kathmandu, I flew home to my wife, Suchi. I welcomed the chance for more rest, and I was grateful that my secret and job were safe. A few days later, I was back at work with the military. Once again, I kicked in doors and took down bad guys, counting the days until it was time to climb another mountain.

CHAPTER 6

SETTING RECORDS

BY THE TIME MAY 2017 CAME AROUND, I HAD BEEN confirmed as a member of the G200E climbing team. I would serve as a team instructor. A second attempt at the world's tallest peak was back on. Because I was going as a member of the British Armed Forces, my expenses would be paid, and I intended to experience every last drop of adventure.

For a while, I'd been thinking about climbing Everest and the neighboring peak of Lhotse, then taking on nearby Makalu, and doing all three in a two-week period. Then I decided I had it in me to climb them in about one week—even though all three mountains were included as some of the world's tallest—all above 26,000 feet (8,000 m). This meant that I would have to move quickly after the G200E climb, descending Everest at record speed to move on to Lhotse. If everything worked out as planned, I could meet with my fellow Gurkha brothers in Kathmandu before taking on the third mountain, Makalu.

I was ready for the challenge. The way I'd made it to the tops of Everest and Dhaulagiri had reaffirmed my hunch that I was a strong high-altitude mountain climber. But it wasn't simply about physical strength. My mindset felt different, too. I had an unending drive to climb.

> BUT IT WASN'T SIMPLY ABOUT PHYSICAL STRENGTH. MY MINDSET FELT DIFFERENT, TOO. I HAD AN UNENDING DRIVE TO CLIMB.

The G200E team traveled to Nepal in April 2017. Once we'd arrived at Everest, our group was divided into two sections. My first job was to guide one of them through the altitude acclimation process that was required to reach the summit. This process took the expedition into Camp 1 and then to Camps 2 and 3. From there we would return to Base Camp, by which point everyone should have been physically primed for a summit push.

During our acclimation process it was clear which climbers were making serious headway and which ones were fading, so I decided to take the strongest on to Camp 2 and then Camp 3, while the slower team members rested at Camp 1 for an extra day. After completing their respective climbs, the two teams took a couple of days to rest in the nearby town of Namche Bazaar. Then, briefing day arrived in Base Camp—the moment when the groups would be organized into two expedition units.

Team A was set to lead the climb. Team B would start their ascent once the first group had summited. When the two parties for our historic expedition were revealed, we discovered that the slower, struggling leaders would go first. Meanwhile, most of the stronger climbers, myself included, and two Gurkha Special Forces instructors, were set to follow on as Team B. For some reason, we'd been placed at the back of the line. I was upset. *We'd earned the right.*

"Why are the fastest climbers not in the lead party?" I asked. "Your mission, the mission of the British government, is to put the first serving Gurkha on the summit. But the strongest have been put to the back."

The room fell silent; there wasn't a lot for anyone to say. Team A was made up of slower leaders with a handful of Gurkhas chucked in. One of Team A's members tried to end the dispute by claiming that everybody was now fully acclimated and equally strong, but I wasn't convinced.

"I saw you all at Camp 1 during the acclimation rotations," I said. "You were struggling to keep up. How can you lead the strongest members when you are slower than them? What happens if a rescue situation kicks off?"

I was frustrated, but there was nothing I could do.

Tensions had been running high for days, probably because the mission was looking like it might not happen. The weather conditions on Everest had been horrific. High winds ravaged everything above Camp 2, and a series of storms was due to roll in within a week. Then, 24 hours prior to us setting off for the summit push, it was announced that some of the fixed lines still weren't in place. The team charged with setting the last of the rope had given up.

The mood grew bleak, especially since this was our second attempt at getting the job done, taking into account the tragedy of 2015. If the decision was made to abandon our climb, there was a risk we might not get another chance. Somehow, we had to make it happen.

When I scanned through the climbing order again, I realized I was the only person on the mountain who could take on the responsibility of fixing the lines. I had the experience and the capability to function in extreme temperatures. As an elite military operator, I knew I had the resilience to nail the mission.

Who else could they rely on?

"I'll go up and set the ropes," I announced.

Most of the guys around me had assumed the mission was effectively over. They seemed pleasantly taken aback at my offer. By this time, everybody on the G200E team knew about my mountaineering skills and the fact that I'd scaled two of the world's highest peaks already, one of which was Everest. Even my rescue of Seema was now common knowledge.

"Trust me, I can do it," I continued.

Eventually, the G200E leaders agreed with my plan. I would lead a fixing team, which included two Special Forces operators, both of whom were Gurkhas, and eight Sherpa guides. The expedition schedule was also changed. If our against-the-odds line-fixing mission ended up being successful, it was decided that the majority of climbers would switch to Team A. While they climbed, Team B would wait at Base Camp, only moving up once the first group had summited.

The pressure was high, but I felt confident, climbing steadily by using the trailblazing techniques I'd first learned on Dhaulagiri. We worked comfortably to Camp 2, sleeping overnight before heading to Camp 4. Having rested briefly, we then made our summit push, and, keen to lead by example, I climbed alone from Camp 4 to the Balcony, the area where the lines had been set.

The sun was up. As we worked across the South Summit and, later, the Hillary Step, it was impossible not to be in awe of the views of Nepal and Tibet around me. But I had no time to stop. As the leader of a line-fixing team, I knew that if we were unable to set these last few ropes, the entire expedition would collapse.

Luckily, my stamina hadn't faded. Around 33 feet (10 m) from the peak, as some of the slower guys in the line-fixing crew caught up, I held back from making the final push alone. *Brothers*, I thought, *we're doing Everest as a team.*

Once everyone was together, we put our arms around one another's shoulders, making the last steps together.

This was history. We had set the fixed lines, and 13 soldiers from the regiment eventually made it to the top during the G200E. (Our ropes would also provide a route for climbers on Everest at the end of that season.) For some of the guys, the climb was a clearly defined endgame, a challenge that couldn't be topped. Where else would they go next? But I was a million miles away from closure. When I looked across at the mountain ranges below me, I knew the next phase of my adventure was waiting.

I WAS READY. AS THE ONLY DESIGNATED INSTRUCTOR WITH the stamina to climb the peak back-to-back, I was to help Team B to the top of Everest. I would need support. A Sherpa guide had been called in for each of my summit attempts, and several oxygen cylinders had been distributed across the mountains for me. But all my plans came crashing down shortly afterward. As I prepared for my second peak of the day, word filtered through that the lines on Lhotse, the next mountain I wanted to climb, were also incomplete. Having experienced the same weather conditions as the team on Everest, the fixing crew had temporarily halted their work shortly after Camp 4.

Even worse, the Sherpa with whom I was supposed to be climbing Lhotse was sick and already descending to Base Camp.

I moved from tent to tent trying to convince one of the other guides to join me, but everyone seemed unable to make another summit push in such a short amount of time.

My heart sank. Climbing Lhotse solo for the first time was probably beyond me, and one mistake would destroy the hopes of Team B waiting at Everest Base Camp. They needed me to lead them to the summit. I was determined not to abandon them after they had worked so hard to achieve their dream of scaling Everest with the G200E. I packed up and headed down.

By the time I reached Camp 2 and rested overnight, it was announced that Team A had made it to the top, around 18 hours after I'd finished my Everest summit. I felt triumphant; our efforts had been worth it. But in a heartbeat, the good news was over-shadowed by some bad. It was decided that the expedition was effectively over. Because a number of Gurkhas serving on Team A had already summited, the mission had been declared complete. It was decided that the climbing should stop. The guys at Base Camp still waiting for their chance were being sent home. This felt like a really selfish decision. These guys had sacrificed their time, money, and more to be here. When I later met up with Team B, the scene was heartbreaking. A few of the guys were in tears.

In the aftermath, it dawned on me that had everything gone according to plan—had the original fixing team done their job, and had the original Team A made it to Everest's peak—my role in Team B would have been redundant, too. I would have been stuck at Base Camp with the others.

A few days later I was back in Kathmandu. My first attempt at Lhotse had been written off, but I was now hearing that the fixed lines had been set all the way to the top. This meant my original goal of climbing Everest and then Lhotse and Makalu in a two-week window was back on, but the timing was really tight.

I planned my routes along the three peaks, estimating I'd need some luck with the weather to nail the schedule. I'd first work my way up to Everest's Camp 3, climbing across to the summit of Lhotse. I'd then backtrack to scale Everest. Once that was done, I could then travel over to Makalu's Base Camp via helicopter.

This was a huge test of endurance, but logistically I had zero concerns. My oxygen was already in place and I could scoop up the oxygen cylinders as I worked my way across the mountains. Plus, the Sherpas I'd booked for the initial attempt were still happy to climb. Everything was set. But then, disaster struck.

When I arrived at the foot of Everest a day or so later, I noticed a cluster of oxygen cylinders on the ground alongside a pile of other discarded equipment from the G200E. When I looked closely, I realized the bottled air was mine. A Sherpa, having wrongly assumed that I'd decided to pack up and head home, had brought some of my air down from one of the camps.

I was angry, but I needed time to think. I was close to being overloaded with equipment and oxygen bottles for my next climb. I didn't have the space for the extra air I needed, but I knew I had air waiting for me at two more camps across the mountain. I was going to climb. However, as I ascended to Everest Camp 2 and then Camp 4 at Lhotse, it was clear that nearly all of my oxygen was gone. I searched the tents and scrabbled around in the freshly dumped snow.

Someone had stolen it.

I was furious. Climbing without air would go against the principles I'd set for myself following Seema's rescue. Yes, I had the strength to scale Lhotse, Everest, and Makalu anyway, but if I started undervaluing the promises I'd made, the process would become habitual and I'd never hit my targets.

Get it together, Nims. Stay tough, bro. You are different—you will find a solution to this problem.

Drawing in some settling breaths, I visualized my oxygen going to a better place. I forced myself to believe the cylinders had been swiped to save the life of another climber. *Someone has survived because of your oxygen, Nims.* Having emotionally reset, I adapted to the situation and tweaked my schedule to move on. My plan was now to top Everest first, in what was shaping up to be a stormy event. I'd then climb Lhotse, where I'd arranged for a friend to drop some bottled air for me at Camp 4. Then, finally I'd climb Makalu.

The wind howled around me and for a brief moment, I had a feeling of self-doubt. What I was about to attempt was huge. *But could I make it?*

I steadied myself.

Yeah. You can.

On May 22, I scaled Everest. The mountain was at its most vicious. Hurricane-force winds swirled at the peak; shards of ice struck me like bullets. The conditions were so severe that a number of other climbers died that day. Leaning into the wind blasts, and knowing that my speed would help me, I worked as quickly as I could with my Sherpa. We both feared for our fingers and toes in the cold as we waited for 45 minutes at the Hillary Step. There was a traffic jam of climbers moving up and down its face to the peak. After I reached the top, I climbed over to Lhotse with a new Sherpa. We pushed on to Camp 4. At the summit of Lhotse, I looked at my watch. I'd been climbing for 10 hours and

15 minutes. Now only Makalu remained untested.

Full disclosure: At that point I had no idea that I had broken the world record for climbing Everest and Lhotse in such quick succession. That wasn't my goal. I only wanted to top the three peaks. When I was told at Base Camp that the previous best had been 20 hours, I was shocked. I'd accidentally cut nearly 10 hours from the fastest registered time.

> AT THAT POINT I HAD NO IDEA THAT I HAD BROKEN THE WORLD RECORD FOR CLIMBING EVEREST AND LHOTSE IN SUCH QUICK SUCCESSION.

Another record was in reach. If I could climb Makalu in the next few days, I'd break the world record for the quickest time taken to top Everest, Lhotse, and Makalu. I was then informed that nobody had ever climbed Everest twice plus Lhotse and Makalu in one climbing season. I liked my chances, even though I'd never climbed Makalu at that point. It was the fifth highest mountain in the world. I had a helicopter set to take me to the next Base Camp, piloted by my good mate Nishal, one of the best high-altitude pilots around. I buzzed with excitement at the potential of what was within reach.

"Brother, you've just smashed a world record," said Nishal, hugging me at the landing zone.

"Yeah, and I can get another one at Makalu."

I wanted to rush my next steps, but Nishal was keen to put my achievements into perspective. "Mate, you said you'd do all three mountains in fourteen days," he said. "You've got a few days to crack Makalu and still catch your flight home with the G200E guys. Why don't you enjoy the moment?"

He then pointed out that May 29 was coming up. It was an event in the Himalaya known as Everest Day. The celebration marked the first ever summit of the mountain in 1953 by Sherpa Tenzing Norgay and Sir Edmund Hillary.

Realizing I could celebrate Everest Day and still have time for the world record, I agreed. I was on vacation after all.

After the festivities, I headed for Makalu. On May 24, I blasted up it. I made it to the peak, all 27,838 feet (8,485 m) in one hit. I led from the front with my small team and trailblazed through heavy snow, high wind, and disorientating cloud cover until I'd reached the top. This in itself was an achievement. Nobody had climbed Makalu that season. A number of teams had made attempts, only to be pushed back by the treacherous conditions.

I had broken two world records: climbing Everest and Lhotse in 10 hours, 15 minutes, and then topping Everest, Lhotse, and Makalu in five days. I was also the first person to climb Everest twice, then Lhotse, and Makalu in the same season.

I made my flight back home with my G200E brothers and was back in England in one piece. But I didn't feel done.

CHAPTER 7

THE NEXT LEVEL

DIDN'T KNOW HOW I'D BEEN ABLE TO CLIMB THREE incredibly challenging peaks so fast without a period of recovery in between. I didn't know why my body didn't wear out. For some reason, I had the physical ability to climb and descend, *climb and descend*, fixing lines and leading expeditions over and over and over. My reserves felt limitless. Above 26,000 feet (8,000 m), I could rally the self-confidence required to take me to the peak of any mountain in the world, whatever the conditions.

I understood my strengths and limitations, and I knew how to use them to my advantage. This allowed me to avoid trouble—for the most part.

Soon after my three climbs, I decided to up my game. If I could take three of the world's largest mountains in five days, maybe I had it in me to climb the five tallest peaks in an equally impressive time: Everest, K2, Kanchenjunga, Lhotse, and Makalu in, say, 80 days? The idea gnawed at me for weeks until I decided to act on it.

There would be hurdles; I knew that. My chances of securing the leave needed to take on such an ambitious project were slim, but I was going to give it a shot anyway. When I made my request, I tried to be convincing. I reminded the senior officer of my outstanding record, in and out of combat, and my growing climbing expertise. I used my work with the G200E as leverage.

My senior officer glanced skeptically at the expedition plan.

"Climbing K2, Nims? One in four people die there. On Kanchenjunga it's one in seven," he said. "This is such a huge project. And it's not as if you're climbing one mountain here. You're running up mountain after mountain in eleven or twelve weeks. Is this even possible?"

There was no way he could authorize so much leave, he explained. It was too risky. Also, if it became known that a Special Forces operator was climbing K2, which was located on the border of Pakistan and China, it might invite a terrorist attack. "It's just not doable, Nims," he said.

I felt deflated, but I wasn't going to abandon my dream. I kept trying for months to get the leave time I needed. When the answer was still no, I decided to take matters into my own hands.

Well, that's it then, I thought. *I'm going to quit.*

Reaching the decision to resign from the military made me feel liberated. I was 35 years old and had given myself the opportunity to think bigger and more boldly about climbing challenges I wanted to take on. Rather than climbing the five tallest mountains in 80 days, what was stopping me from topping all 14 Death Zone mountains in the quickest time imaginable?

It was in the Gurkha blood to be fearless, so while there was every chance an avalanche might sweep me away on Annapurna, the 10th highest mountain in the world, I wasn't going to stress about it too much. Meanwhile, the dangers involved in climbing all 14 Death Zone peaks were manageable. I'd learned how to work in poor weather and deep snow; I could operate effectively, without fear.

Then there were all the logistics: paperwork and permit requests, particularly from the Chinese and Tibetan authorities. It was also very expensive. It would cost more than a million dollars to climb all 14 mountains. But I would figure it out. If I believed that my goal of climbing the 14 mountain peaks, all over 26,000 feet (8,000 m), in quick succession was achievable, then it was achievable. Every part of my training and combat experience had told me so. Now it was time to figure out how to plan a series of high-altitude expeditions. I'd built up plenty of connections in the climbing community, so I got to work.

I flipped open my laptop at home one afternoon, hoping to understand how long an expedition of this kind might take. A brief search online told me that only about 40 other mountaineers had managed to climb the 14 tallest peaks. The field was small but impressive. And the fastest any of them had climbed all 14 was just under eight years.

Judging by the way I'd worked through Everest, Lhotse, and Makalu in five days and Dhaulagiri in two weeks, I believed it was within my reach to go quicker. The only question was by how much.

I sat down to figure it out. I listed the mountains I needed to climb and what the setbacks might be, from how long it would take to get permits to weather conditions that might derail my goal. With all that in mind, I decided I could climb all 14 Death Zone peaks in seven months. That meant shaving seven years off the world record. It was ambitious, but I grew into the idea.

The bottom line was to climb as quickly as possible, whatever the weather, Nims style. With these climbs, I also wanted to alert the world to the region's floods and disappearing glaciers. And I wanted to shine a spotlight on the plight of those people living and working within the mountain communities. It was a way I could help the region and my home country of Nepal.

Most of all, though, I loved the thought of ripping up the rule book. If I could show kids and adults alike what was humanly possible, maybe my far-fetched ambitions would inspire others to think big and to push themselves in ways they never thought were possible. Plus, I'd have an incredible story to remember.

> MOST OF ALL, THOUGH, I LOVED THE THOUGHT OF RIPPING UP THE RULE BOOK.

I gave my grand mission a name: *Project Possible*. Then I prepared a plan.

LEAVING THE SPECIAL BOAT SERVICE WOULDN'T BE EASY. There was a sense of security being part of a team, and for 16 years, the British military had been my all. They'd told me where to be and when, and they'd provided me with a house and a daily routine. Yes, the job was dangerous and highly stressful, but there were some comforting familiarities to it. I had structure, focus, and loyalty. There was also a steady paycheck.

Quitting meant giving up all of it, but I put aside my doubts. On March 19, 2018, I submitted my resignation request, giving one year notice. At first some friends in the squadron tried to change my mind, and so did my commanders. I was promoted to a new position, offered a job in a new department, and warned that if I left, I'd be giving up good pay and benefits. As I drove away from the barracks after receiving the new job offer and listening to my commanders' warnings, I second-guessed myself. *What should I do?* But in the end, I stuck with my original plan: I wanted to climb the big mountains.

As for the money, I had grown up poor in Nepal. If I really had to, living in a tent for the rest of my life would have posed no problems at all.

My friends and family seemed confused about my decision. When I announced the news, they were upset. To them, this was a baffling career change, and a risky one financially.

Since joining the Gurkhas, I had sent my parents money every month. They mean the world to me. Also, my mom had recently become very ill.

She was suffering from a heart condition, and at one point had to undergo surgery to insert a stent. This was followed by kidney failure, and Mom often had to visit the hospital for treatment. Eventually, she was placed in a permanent facility in Kathmandu. (There wasn't a suitable clinic in our hometown of Chitwan.) My dad, half paralyzed, was unable to visit her in the city, and it had become my ultimate goal to bring them together again in the same house. But with Project Possible now underway, all that would be paused for now. My mom was also worried about me going on 14 climbs.

Mom wanted to know what my new plan entailed.

"So, you know the fourteen biggest mountains in the world, Mom?"

She nodded. "Some of them."

Mom listed a few names. "Everest, Dhaulagiri. Oh, and Annapurna. But what has that got to do with you?"

I told her my plan was to climb all of them. "I'm going to do this. I'm going to show the world what I am capable of—what we can all do—if we put our minds to it. And I'm going to come back stronger. I'll be a different Nims."

She smiled. "You don't listen to what we tell you anyway, so I know you're not going to do what we say. Our blessings are with you."

My family's concerns weren't the only hurdle, however. Friends laughed whenever I talked about Project Possible. That was fair enough. The goal was supposed to be tough, unrealistic even, but only because nobody had achieved anything quite like it before. But then, space travel and the four-minute mile had both been considered impossible before they were achieved, too. If somebody had informed a young Neil Armstrong that his dream wasn't possible, would he have listened? *No way.*

Of course, there was a chance I might fail, but there was also a chance I could pull it off. It was a chance I wanted to take.

CHAPTER 8

MAKING IT HAPPEN

FROM THE MINUTE MY RESIGNATION NOTICE WAS accepted by the military, I set two plans in motion. The first was to organize my team for Project Possible. I pulled together a group of Nepali climbers whom I knew would be up to the task of supporting me over the seven months and 14 peaks. I then figured out which mountains to climb, and when, using weather reports of the past five climbing seasons.

I also decided to split Project Possible into three phases based on the landscape of each mountain. The first was to take place in Nepal. My plan was to crash through Annapurna, Dhaulagiri, Kanchenjunga, Everest, Lhotse, and Makalu in April and May of 2019. This would be followed by the Pakistani mountains of Nanga Parbat, Gasherbrum I and II, K2, and Broad Peak in July. Finally, I would return to Nepal for Manaslu in the fall, before heading to Tibet to top Cho Oyu and Shishapangma.

The second part of the organization process was trickier. I needed to gather together the money necessary to make these climbs happen. I needed help.

I'd learned that to fund projects of this nature I would have to rely on a series of sponsorship deals, in which companies financed my trip in return for exposure and branding opportunities that arose whenever I topped one of the 14 peaks. Some extra cash would come from taking experienced mountaineers with me to the peaks of one mountain from each phase.

The work was relentless. While I planned the 14 expeditions throughout 2018, a friend worked on securing the financing. While finishing up my stint in the military, I fit in meetings and planning sessions. I was running on fumes seven days a week. I approached every day with a positive thought: *I can do this. I will navigate just about every problem the mission might throw at me. I've already climbed the world's tallest peak. The only thing standing in my way right now is funding. Get out there and smash it.*

In addition to the funding my friend had secured, I gave my all to raising money. I wanted to make my dream happen.

I knew that I had to present Project Possible as something worth sponsoring. It was important to make some bold statement about the mission, something that would generate headlines and get people talking.

I announced my intention to establish even more records. The first one, obviously, was the speed at which I intended to climb the 14 mountains. I also announced that I would try to beat my personal best time on Everest, Lhotse, and Makalu (and my time from the summit of Everest to the summit of Lhotse). I said that I intended to break the world's quickest time for climbing the Pakistan Death Zone mountains, too, as well as for climbing the top five highest mountains in the world: Kanchenjunga, Everest, Lhotse, Makalu, and K2.

After several months spent on a conveyor belt of meetings and phone calls, I was dealt a crushing blow.

"Nims, we've raised barely any money," said my associate, sadly. "It's not looking good."

I was in trouble. Or so I thought. I immediately switched my tactics and decided to raise money myself. Most mornings I got up at 4 a.m. and worked on my social media outreach for a few hours before racing to the 7 a.m. train into London. Usually, I'd attend around four or five meetings a day. On the rare occasions when my work was done before midnight, I'd open up my computer to write a series of follow-up emails. Then, I'd round off the day with another session on Instagram or Facebook.

The work felt like a grind, and it was frustrating. Next to nothing in the way of cash arrived for a couple of months. By the time 2019 rolled around, with my clock ticking, I still hadn't convinced potential sponsors of my abilities or the significance of the project. Meetings often ended with a thanks-but-no-thanks dismissal. But I found it impossible to slow down, because I was carrying so much desire for my mission. The thought of quitting never entered my mind. I had faith. But at times keeping that faith would prove to be hard work.

AFTER EXHAUSTING ALMOST EVERY RESOURCE AND getting no after no, I finally had some success. I was able to raise money here and there by making connections through military friends, speaking at a corporate event, and gaining clients to take with me on my climbs. But it wasn't enough. I had to do something more drastic. I had to take money out of our house.

I spoke to my wife. I needed her blessing to take this risky next step.

After everything I'd put her through, from fighting in a dangerous job abroad for several years to retiring from work early and turning down a retirement income in order to climb mountains, this was a bold thing to ask. But I was out of options.

Suchi looked at me sternly. "Okay, Nims," she said. "But you better be right."

It was reassuring to know that she still believed in me and had faith in Project Possible. She told me that there was zero doubt in her mind that I'd succeed in the mission once it was up and running. I was grateful for her. For my dream, she was prepared to risk everything.

BORROWING AGAINST THE VALUE OF OUR HOUSE WAS A big step, but it still didn't yield enough money. There was a moment or two when I nearly crumbled during the fundraising drive. But my faith was restored yet again.

I heard that the U.K.'s Nepali community and a group of retired Gurkhas had organized a Project Possible fundraising drive. Retirees and veterans were making donations. The gesture was incredibly humbling. As the countdown to my first climb approached, I'd raised around $160,000 from various income streams. This was barely enough to cover Phase One of the project, but I expected more interest to arrive with every climb. I had what I needed to start my journey.

I readied myself for the most ambitious operation of my life.

CHAPTER 9

ANNAPURNA, THE START OF PHASE ONE

WHILE I COULD HAVE STARTED ON ONE OF THE less intimidating climbs in the region, I chose to begin with Annapurna. Climbing this mountain would give me the opportunity to assess my expedition team. To climb any mountain higher than 26,000 feet (8,000 m), an experienced mountaineer requires a support crew. It was critical for me to discover how effective my crew could be. I needed to know which individuals I could trust to keep their head in the game, no matter how dangerous things got. I also wanted to discover any weak links within the group, if there were any at all. On Annapurna, potential death awaited us at every stage, and there was no easy path to the top. It would provide a good test of our team.

From the outset, I made it clear that it would be my job to run the team, to make decisions under pressure, and to use all the skills I'd learned on the mountain and in the military. In the

Special Forces, each team was made up of expert warriors. My aim had been to build the same kind of climbing group. Sure, I was team leader, but the others would be operating as specialist climbers; each of them possessed expert skills, and they were capable of looking after themselves in moments of high stress.

I wanted us to trailblaze through the deepest snow and into the hardest weather toward the 14 summits. I wanted us to become elite—to be regarded as the Special Forces of high-altitude mountaineering.

I was also looking for different qualities in different people, as I intended to split the expedition into two groups based on who fit what role best. The first group was the core team to lead the climb: two Sherpas, Mingma David and Geljen Sherpa; Gesman Tamang, a strong but relatively inexperienced climber; and Lakpa Dendi Sherpa. I would also have a secondary group on hand to provide backup if necessary: Sonam Sherpa, Halung Dorchi Sherpa, Ramesh Gurung, and Mingma's brother, Kasang Sherpa. I also wanted one team member in place to double-check all my expedition plans as we went along: Dawa Sherpa. I was happy with this setup, and I knew who should be in which group. I had a team full of great Sherpa climbers. My goal was to help them gain experience and credibility in order to earn more money in their line of work. They were diligent and hardworking, and they deserved to be recognized and compensated well for what they did.

WE ARRIVED AT ANNAPURNA'S BASE CAMP ON MARCH 28, 2019. Once there, I noticed a shared mentality was building among the team. Everyone worked hard and nobody complained if the effort looked like it was becoming too rough, as it so often did on the mountains.

Whenever I tweaked our plan for Annapurna, others offered ideas. Every idea was tested and nothing was dismissed. Plenty of that had to do with our team spirit, but a number of the guys had heard about my previous efforts on Everest, Lhotse, and Makalu. I'd earned their respect and they were in the process of earning mine. This was exactly the mentality we needed if Phase One were to succeed.

A day or so before we began our first rope-fixing climb, the team performed a puja, a Nepali ceremony conducted with a lama, or spiritual leader. During the puja the group offered prayers to the mountain gods. Juniper was lit, rice was thrown, and a mast of prayer flags was raised. The hope was that those same gods might grant us safe passage to the peak, sparing us from the wrath of an avalanche or crevasse fall.

While I'm not dedicated to one god, I believe in the power of prayer. I also like to connect with nature alone, so once the puja was completed, I took myself away from the group to stare up at Annapurna's summit. The sky was a bright blue; thick clouds drifted around the higher edges, but I was locked into a one-to-one conversation with the wall of rock and ice ahead. In a way, I wanted to ask the mountain for permission.

Okay, can I? Or can I not?

Having watched and waited, I sensed hope.

The route we were taking was a monster: a line over Annapurna's north face, an intimidating climb that was first scaled by the French climber Maurice Herzog in 1950. We were ready to go. On April 2, 2019, accompanied by Mingma and

Geljen, I pressed ahead with confidence. We made up the line-fixing team, and we were eager to execute the first stage in our mission, which was to set the ropes up to Camps 1 and 2.

The way up was unforgiving. Initially, the path led us through a snow-covered field of rocks that a climber could negotiate without too much trouble, but beyond that, the route became sketchy. The landscape was cracked by deep crevasses. Some of them were visible; others had been hidden below a carpet of thick snow. One wrong step would make a climber fall to his death, so it was important that all of us were roped up. If somebody slipped through the snow, the weight of the remaining mountaineers, bracing as a group, would hopefully stop their fall.

Before long, we had climbed high above Base Camp, but the weather conditions had worsened. As we anchored ropes and fixed lines, a heavy wind whipped around us in a fury. The snow was soon packed into waist-deep drifts, and the work became a grind. It was my job as point man to drag the other team members along. I lifted my legs high and planted my boots firmly, with focus, so that the others could fall in behind me. All the while, I was listening out for the telltale rumblings of an oncoming avalanche. With every step, I reminded myself that I was strong. There was no doubt I'd eventually reach the summit, but avalanches were uncontrollable events that nobody could really prepare for.

I felt the crunch of snow under my boots and the icy burn of oxygen in my lungs. We climbed, slowly and steadily.

CHAPTER 10

AVALANCHE!

FTER HOURS AND HOURS OF HEAVY WORK, HAVING trailblazed through miles of knee-deep snow, the Project Possible team walked into Camp 2. We'd tackled steep ribs and buttresses and made it through a series of crevasses along the way. It was grinding, but with the fixed lines in place, we were closer to being primed for our eventual summit push. We still had much to climb, but despite the fatigue, everybody seemed to be in high spirits. The strong winds had died down and the mountain felt much calmer. The sun was setting, and the group danced and joked. The smell of fried chicken and rice wafted over the camp.

Then there was a crack, like thunder, from somewhere above us.

Oh no ... avalanche!

It was a big one. A large chunk of Annapurna's north face had sheared away, and an eruption of white was billowing down the mountain at an unstoppable speed. For a split second I seemed unable to react, paralyzed at the magnitude of what was about to happen. Everything in the avalanche's path was in danger of being crushed. And we were very much in the avalanche's path. There was no way of escaping it.

> EVERYTHING IN THE AVALANCHE'S PATH WAS IN DANGER OF BEING CRUSHED. AND WE WERE VERY MUCH IN THE AVALANCHE'S PATH.

Move!

"Everybody into the shelters!" I shouted.

I'd often been told that it was always best to seek some form of protection in the event of an avalanche. Even something as flimsy as a tent would do. *Well, it was better than nothing.* Acting on instinct, I ran for the nearest one and dived inside. My teammates Sonam and Mingma bundled in behind me, zipping up the door. Readying ourselves for impact, we huddled together, shoulder to shoulder, the avalanche's roar growing ever louder as the ground trembled around us. Escaping the chaos seemed unlikely. Suspecting we might have to cut our way out of the tent, fast, once we'd been smothered, I shouted instructions to the others.

"Mingma, get your knife. Sonam, back yourself against the tent poles and brace."

But Sonam looked broken. He was mumbling a prayer to the mountain gods. I felt another shiver of fear. *This is bad.*

There was a moment of wishful thinking. *I hope that prayer works, Sonam.* Only God knows how much snow smashed over us at full force, hammering and tearing at the tent. For several seconds the fabric seemed to buck without breaking. I expected to be swept down the mountain at any second, all of us tumbling over each other. But suddenly, and unexpectedly, everything became still. There was silence. Then I heard the sound of pan-icked breathing. We'd survived.

"Sonam, are you cool?" I asked, pulling him closer, shaking him gently.

He nodded. Around us, the mountain felt eerily calm. When I left the tent to survey the wreckage of Camp 2 and check on our supplies and equipment, it was clear we'd been lucky. Only the tail end of the violent event had caught us. Nobody was hurt, and nothing had been destroyed. But the mood was very uneasy among the local Sherpas, who were in place to assist with our line-fixing efforts.

With the last of the daylight fading, the local Sherpas fear-fully trudged back to Base Camp. Our goal of fixing the lines to Camps 3 and 4 had become much more daunting than before, but at least we were still alive. Picking apart our options in the darkness, I sensed the usual route was now too dangerous. Every step was an avalanche waiting to happen.

I stared up at Annapurna's peak and asked the question yet again.

Okay, can I? Or can I not?

Then I joined the others for dinner, hoping the mountain might behave more mercifully from then on.

I WOKE WITH THE SUNRISE—AND A PLAN.

As part of the expedition inventory, I'd packed a few pieces of camera equipment. For a long while I'd wanted to film a lot of Project Possible as we moved from mountain to mountain. My aim was to film as much as I could while I was climbing. Even though I had next to no filmmaking experience, I was confident I could capture plenty of exciting material. Eventually, I hoped to show my expeditions to the world by making a documentary, or maybe presenting a live talk or two, but I also wanted to silence any doubters who would inevitably pop up once the operation was done.

I intended to make it home with as much footage as I could. I brought along two guys to help with the editing and social media: Sagar and Alit Gurung. They had shown so much faith in Project Possible that they had resigned from their jobs in the U.K. to join us.

Before starting our climb from Base Camp on day one, I'd distributed headcams to everyone on the team. We had a hand-held digital camera on standby, too. But the most exciting tool in my filming inventory was a drone. Of course, it would be great for filming aerial shots as we climbed. But it was also a useful tool to scope out the terrain of the mountains. As we planned our best route up Annapurna's avalanche-ravaged terrain, I was struck by an idea.

In the same way that the British military used drones to improve the tactical understanding of a battle space, I'd be able to fly one across Annapurna, working out the safest route toward Camp 3. Mingma, Sonam, and I hovered the drone over a series of icy ridges, assessing the captured footage on a phone for a new route up. And there it was!

A long, vertical ridge that ran directly above us had come into view. Dusted in snow, it resembled the bridge of a sharp angular nose from a distance, and I recognized it as the notorious Dutch Rib, a knife-edge of powder and ice. Very few people had attempted it, probably because the route appeared so daunting.

But by the looks of things, there was just enough width on the nose's bridge for us to advance upward.

The work would be challenging, mainly because anyone scaling it was bound to be exposed. If a climber slipped on the compacted rock and ice, there would be nothing to break his long, painful ride to the bottom.

When I returned to Base Camp later that day and announced my plan to the waiting expeditions, I was told that the Dutch Rib was a no-go zone. One Sherpa, an Annapurna guide with years of experience, instantly knocked back the idea. "Nobody's climbed that route for years," he said. "It's too hard."

His reaction unsettled me a little bit.

My military training had instilled a sense of inner positivity; it was often my job to find creative solutions to sketchy problems. I assessed the Dutch Rib drone footage once more and decided to put that theory into practice, figuring, *What the heck?* I decided to go ahead and fix the ropes over the Dutch Rib the next day. As the leader of the line-fixing team, I was merely giving them an option. It was up to them whether they took it or not.

After a full day on the Dutch Rib, the work had been rough, and with the light fading, I found myself caught between Camps 2 and 3. Moving up in the darkness on such a dangerous slope seemed risky, so we had to stay put for the night. We fixed our tent to the nose's bridge with around 30 anchors. Geljen and I rested above a sheer drop that would have meant certain death had either one of us rolled over during our sleep.

AFTER PROGRESSING ALONG THE DUTCH RIB AND SETTING the fixed lines to Camp 3, we returned to Base Camp, readying the expedition team and accompanying Sherpas for our summit push. A plan was set: I would lead the way with Mingma, climbing one day ahead of our clients. They would be guided through the camps by Sonam—all of them following our deep footfalls in the snow. The fixing team intended to push to Camp 2 and sleep overnight. A day later, we'd scale the Dutch Rib, resting at Camp 3 before setting the lines to Camp 4. From there, we could expect to spend a full day trailblazing through the deep snow while anchoring lines to the mountain.

If everything went according to plan, our expedition team, plus the other parties climbing Annapurna that day, would probably meet us at Camp 4 shortly after the last of the lines had been set. Then we'd be able to climb to the very top as a group.

This was the first summit push of the mission. I was ready.

After two days of solid work, we were able to rest at Camp 4 for a few hours as the other parties caught up to our position. I was tired, but there was plenty of energy left in the tank as I kicked back in my tent. Then, I was suddenly struck with an idea. I wanted to make the final push to the top without oxygen. To scale these mountains without it had long been considered the purest form of mountaineering. It would also silence critics who thought oxygen shouldn't be used.

THEN, I WAS SUDDENLY STRUCK WITH AN IDEA. I WANTED TO MAKE THE FINAL PUSH TO THE TOP WITHOUT OXYGEN.

I mentioned my plan to Mingma in our tent; he shook his head. He worried the mission might lose its momentum if I wasn't able to power forward at my usual speed.

↑ **MY HOME IN DANA,** where I was born. I am sitting on my mom's lap and my father is behind us.

→ **THE PURJA FAMILY.** Two of my older brothers, Ganga and Kamal, joined the Gurkhas. I wanted to follow in their footsteps.

← **JOINING THE GURKHAS** in 2003. Being in their ranks meant everything.

↑ **ONE OF PROJECT POSSIBLE'S** first rescues. We got off to a dramatic start!

→ **TAKING ON ANNAPURNA.** We made it to the top on April 23, 2019.

DHAULAGIRI

2

↑ **DON'T BELIEVE THE BLUE SKIES—**the weather on Dhaulagiri was brutal!

KANCHENJUNGA

→ **WALKING ABOVE THE CLOUDS** at Kanchenjunga, one of the most dangerous mountains in the world.

3

↑ **WITH ONE PHOTO,** I captured the chaos that sometimes kicks off on Everest.

LHOTSE

5

⬆ **PULLING MYSELF ALONG THE FIXED LINES** in the Death Zones takes strength, courage, and belief.

6

MAKALU

24/05/2019 0

⬆ **I HAD NOW CLIMBED SIX NEPALI PEAKS** at a rapid speed. On to Pakistan!

NANGA PARBAT

↑ **NANGA PARBAT WAS DANGEROUS GROUND—**I had to tread carefully, on and off the mountain.

K2

← **K2 WAS A TERRIFYING CHALLENGE** for the other climbers on the mountain. I trailblazed a path to the second highest peak in the world.

G1 & G2

↑ **G1 AND G2 TESTED** me and my GPS to the max.

> **BROAD PEAK**

← **BY CONQUERING BROAD PEAK** I had climbed all five Pakistan 8000ers in 23 days—a new world record!

↑ **STANDING ATOP CHO OYU IN TIBET.** I was so close to completing Project Possible, but the clock was ticking!

→ **WITH CHO OYU BEHIND ME,** another peak was checked off the list.

MANASLU

→ **MANASLU IS A NEPALESE 8,000ER,** one of the most dangerous mountains in the world.

↑ **... BUT WE MADE LIGHT WORK OF IT,** leaving only Shishapangma to climb.

14

↑ **CLIMBING TO THE TOP** of Shishapangma and into the record book. *Boom!*

← **PROJECT POSSIBLE** was my life's greatest achievement ... for now.

↑ **AT THE TOP OF EVEREST** having led the 2017 G200E in horrendous conditions. It was not long after this expedition that I came up with the idea for Project Possible.

← **WITH MUM.** Everything I'd achieved was inspired by her.

"We need your aggression, Nimsdai," he said.

I tried using reason. "I've been leading from the front the whole expedition. I know I can climb any mountain without oxygen."

I knew the chances of him backing down were slim, but I pressed ahead anyway. "Mate, just for the sake of these people and their opinions, let me climb without air."

He laughed. "No, Nimsdai!"

Mingma's opinion was important to me. His uncle and my friend, Dorje, was highly regarded in Nepali climbing. Mingma had also become a very knowledgeable guide in his own right.

I knew Mingma was right. His strong opinion reminded me of a saying I'd once held as a kid hoping to make it into the Gurkhas: *You don't have to prove anything to anyone.* There was also the promise I'd made to myself about always carrying air on the highest peaks. Breaking it might lead to bad habits. Bad habits might result in failure.

So I backed down.

I didn't have time to lose focus. I understood the final push to the top would be brutally hard, even with air. There were around 3,280 feet (1,000 m) to go, and some of the route required us to trailblaze through another blanket of waist-high snow. I'd also have to scale a steep climb through an ice cliff before negotiating a final section of tricky, slippery rock shortly before the peak.

The team departed from Camp 4 at 9 p.m. I realized that most of my route-fixing team were now guiding their private clients, one-on-one, and that the work to come would be intense. By the looks of things, only Mingma and I were available to power through the snow. Realizing that we didn't have enough manpower, I pulled everybody in close.

"Guys, everyone does ten minutes of trailblazing," I said. "Do twenty minutes if you can. Whatever you have in you, use it. When the person leading the team gets too tired, he should stop and move to the side and wait to join the end of the line. The second guy then becomes point man for his ten minutes or so. This will keep our momentum going."

With a clear strategy in place, we set the rope and trailblazed most of the route, each of us taking turns to lead the way until Annapurna's peak was finally in sight. At 3:30 p.m., after climbing through the night, we finally made it.

I took a moment to soak in the view of the jagged teeth of the Himalaya swaddled in clouds below.

The first peak on the list was done, and I remained unbroken.

It was April 23, 2019. A clock was ticking and the world was watching. *My race was on.*

CHAPTER 11

DHAULAGIRI

ROM ANNAPURNA, WE PLANNED TO HEAD TO Kathmandu, and from there to Dhaulagiri's Base Camp. But, so much for plans. When still on Annapurna, we were told a climber needed to be rescued. We helped him get to the Annapurna Base Camp, and then to Kathmandu. This unexpected mission of mercy delayed us, but no matter. We continued moving forward.

Because of this setback in our planned schedule, we missed our best window for climbing Dhaulagiri. A nasty weather system had blown in. A heavy snow dump was burying our fixed lines, and by the sound of it, we weren't going to find them. Meanwhile, our tents on the mountain's higher camps had been beaten down by powerful winds. By all accounts some of the shelters were in shreds. The morale of my team at Base Camp was in equally bad shape. Our supplies were running low, too.

I had to fix this.

Although I understood the importance of climbing Dhaulagiri quickly, the unity within Project Possible's team members was also important. I'd learned that organizing an expedition party was no different from organizing a group of soldiers in war. They needed purpose and incentive, but food and downtime were vital, too. Without periods of rest and recovery, there was every chance that an individual, or the whole team, might fail in the heat of battle. So I told the guys we were withdrawing from the mountain to take a breather. We visited the town of Pokhara for a week. We rode motorbikes, relaxed, and built back our resolve. Our moods were lifted, and we felt ready to go.

On May 10, we started climbing Dhaulagiri. Battling through heavy clouds and winds of more than 40 miles an hour (64 km/h), we reached the summit at 5:30 p.m. on May 12. We dug our way across deep hills of snow to climb a few feet at a time. The effort was exhausting. It certainly wasn't safe, but I knew I had it in me to lead what was proving to be a brave and highly skilled team through the extreme weather. Whenever the wind seemed to die down for the briefest of moments, the team exploded forward, climbing as fast as possible. We would then lean into the storm, bracing ourselves until it was time to move up again.

Whenever the team rested, I allowed them to sit for only five minutes. When time was up, I made sure to be the first one to stand and then to trailblaze. I figured it was best to lead by example. I was eager to move quickly, but I wasn't about to risk the lives of my teammates.

It was soon time to make our descent, and the conditions often threatened to overwhelm us. The mountain was increasingly hostile, and the winds were so powerful that, at

> I FIGURED IT WAS BEST TO LEAD BY EXAMPLE. I WAS EAGER TO MOVE QUICKLY, BUT I WASN'T ABOUT TO RISK THE LIVES OF MY TEAMMATES.

times, it was impossible to see. My eyes burned even though I was wearing protective goggles. As we worked our way to Base Camp, I sensed a shift was taking place. The Project Possible team was discovering a unique bond. Intense loyalties were developing between us because the stakes we were facing were so huge. Surviving the treacherous conditions on Dhaulagiri had brought us all a little bit closer. *The group had my back, and I had theirs.*

We'd need every connection in that bond to hold firm if we were to survive our next mountain: Kanchenjunga.

CHAPTER 12

KANCHENJUNGA

KANCHENJUNGA IS THE THIRD TALLEST MOUNTAIN in the world at more than 28,169 feet (8,586 m). It was also potentially the toughest expedition within Phase One. Kanchenjunga is renowned for being brutally tough to climb; few people have had the resilience, luck, and strength to reach its peak. From Camp 4 to the top, climbers must scale 3,280 more feet (1,000 m), an excruciating grind. Compounding the challenge is deep snow that often smothers the ascent to the shoulder that runs toward Kanchenjunga's peak.

Before we got to Kanchenjunga, we knew that climbers who make it to the final ridge face awful winds and biting cold. Oxygen levels drop to 33 percent, and the terrain is a bewildering minefield of loose rock, ice-covered boulders, and blinding snow-drifts. People who had gone before us said the route feels never-ending, with the summit forever out of reach. Many people turn back long before making it to the top.

I didn't feel overwhelmed by the challenge. We had blitzed the first two mountains in very fast time under incredibly difficult

circumstances, so I knew we had it in us to charge up Kanchenjunga, too. But there was little doubt that everyone in our team
was feeling frazzled after our difficult preparations for this climb.
We spent five days on Dhaulagiri carrying heavy loads of gear on
our backs, fixing lines, and digging up the rope that had been buried by heavy snowfall. We were battle bruised, and we hadn't even
begun the ascent. When we arrived at Kanchenjunga's Base Camp
on May 14, 2019, the team fell into a short period of relaxation,
essential for morale before tackling the mountain. We ate fried
chicken that we bought in a nearby village and took it easy while
we made plans for the next 24 hours.

Rather than resting for a day at Camps 1, 2, 3, and 4, like normal expeditions usually do, we were going to move fast, pushing
immediately to the top in one hit. *No messing around.* We were
already acclimated to high altitude. If our energy levels faded,
stopping and resting would have caused us to fail. I would have
fallen asleep on the spot.

We set out in high spirits and climbed quickly to Camp 1,
spiking our heart rates and shocking our bodies into action.
Below us, crevasses hid under the snow covered terrain. Above,
the lower slopes were notorious for dropping heavy avalanche
payloads and falling rock onto unsuspecting climbers. The
weather held even more dangers.

A number of boulders around us had been frozen together.
Because the sun was high during the day, though, thawing ice
had the potential to trigger a mini avalanche. We decided to take
turns keeping each other safe. One of us would scan the ridges
above for potential bombardments, while the other two sprinted
to the nearest point of shelter. If anybody shouted "Rock!" the
group would dive for cover.

At first, our rapid tactics worked well; our energy levels were high.

By 5 p.m., we were zipping up our summit suits at Camp 1. The expedition parties already on the mountain were into the thick of their respective summit pushes, and at 7 p.m. a lot of them were already leaving Camp 4. In the fading light, I noticed their headlamps flickering high above us, which worried me a little. The distance between the high camp and the peak looked challenging.

As we moved up to Camp 2 and then 3 and beyond on Kanchenjunga, I experienced that familiar rush of anxiety and excitement.

The mountain was a logjam with people moving up and down the rope. Those moving toward the peak seemed to vibrate with urgency, but the mountaineers descending to the lower camps carried a different energy. Many of them were exhausted; others looked stressed. Some climbers even seemed to be teetering on the tipping point between death and survival, having worn themselves out on the way to the summit.

WE SUMMITED KANCHENJUNGA AT NOON ON MAY 15, 2019. Hugging Mingma, I shouted into the clouds excitedly and reached into my rucksack. There were photos to take and flags to unpack. The first one carried the Project Possible logo; another had the Special Boat Service badge printed across it.

"This is it," I shouted, reciting the regiment's motto. "By strength and guile, the only one, SBS!"

From our position, the peaks of Everest, Makalu, and Lhotse were in full view—the final three destinations of Phase One. Somewhere in the distance were the contours that separated Nepal's border from China and India, too. Bright blue skies arced overhead. This was the banner day I'd long dreamed of. When I looked at my watch, there were only a few hours of daylight left. It was time to begin the long walk down, but drama struck almost immediately. An Indian mountaineer and his guide,

> BRIGHT BLUE SKIES ARCED OVERHEAD. THIS WAS THE BANNER DAY I'D LONG DREAMED OF.

whom we'd seen earlier, were stranded below, unable to move.

I tried to rouse them. "What's the problem?" I asked. Some horrible attack of altitude sickness appeared to be overwhelming the mountaineer.

The Sherpa shook his head. "It's his oxygen; it's run out. My air has run out as well. Now this guy can't move down and obviously I can't leave him here, so I'm trying to convince him to come with me, but he's not even moving. He thinks the next step will be his last."

I looked down at the climber. "What's your name, buddy?"

"He's called Biplab," mumbled the guide. "He's stopped talking."

When I checked him over, Biplab was thankfully conscious, but it was hard to tell what was wrong. His Sherpa seemed to be in bad shape, too, but he could at least stand and place one foot in front of the other.

I wasn't going to leave either of them in such an uncertain state. They were unable to save themselves, so it was up to

Mingma, Gesman, and me to get them down. Operating quickly was imperative, though. Some oxygen might be enough to get Biplab on the move, but we all knew that if he was unable to descend, at least to Camp 4, he was probably going to die.

"We're going to get you home," I shouted, helping him to his feet.

Mingma volunteered his oxygen cylinder to Biplab. Because the air was dangerously thin, the shock to Mingma's system would prove debilitating over a number of hours, but for now he was tough enough to support the Sherpa who was getting to his feet.

"Let's use our speed," I suggested. "The only way these people get better is if they get down. Oxygen is the biggest medicine for all of us."

I radioed down to Base Camp for assistance. "Guys, it's Nims," I said. "We've got two stranded climbers up here, and we've given them our oxygen. We're going to conduct a rescue, but we need some more air. Can somebody from Camp 4 help us?"

"Yes, we'll help," shouted a voice. "Three Sherpas are coming to you with oxygen."

I moved closer to check on Biplab, asking if he'd like to speak to anyone on the satellite phone. Although time was against us, I knew that a shot of positivity would help him during what was bound to be a long, tough descent.

"My wife," he said.

Shortly afterward, the couple was connected. By the sound of things, his entire family had gathered around one cell phone, and Biplab was laughing. He'd located the inspiration and sense of positivity that were so important when making it off the mountain in one piece. There was a feeling of relief and hope. For a brief moment, I believed we were going to be okay.

But I was wrong.

Mingma and I grabbed Biplab's arms, Gesman held his feet, and we attached him to our safety rope. Together we started the heavy, painful slog toward Camp 4, but because this was an unexpected rescue operation and we were without our usual supplies, we had to improvise.

The terrain posed a challenging mix of rock, snow, and ice, and the work was slow. We pulled and lifted, the three of us struggling under the weight of Biplab.

Shortly after starting our rescue, I realized another climber was coming toward us on the line, but he was heading up rather than down. *Was it help?* Whoever it was seemed to be working alone and looked seriously ill-equipped for the effort. His every movement seemed labored, and simply clinging on to the line appeared to be an incredible strain. Then I recognized the summit suit. It was Rodrigo, a Chilean climber we met on our way up. He was still moving toward the top, and I felt dread. Because it was midafternoon, there was no way he'd be able to make it to the peak of Kanchenjunga and descend to safety all alone in the darkness.

As he moved closer, I grabbed at him. "Look, brother, you need to go down now. It's nearly two o'clock."

But Rodrigo was still unwilling to listen. His body might have been failing, but his determination seemed unbreakable.

Rodrigo tried to push past me on the line. I recognized the telltale indicators of summit fever, a disorientating condition in which an individual becomes so obsessed with making it to the top of whichever mountain they're climbing that they forget the importance of executing the second part of the mission: getting home. I reckoned Rodrigo had also been spun out by altitude. Without oxygen, his brain was probably unable to process any important information as readily as a climber working lower down the mountain.

I shouted out to him as he moved ahead. "Look, brother, I cannot force you to get down from here now. Please be very, very careful—it's your life on the line."

Then I grabbed the radio and called down to Camp 4, where I knew Rodrigo's expedition operators and camp support were waiting. I'd twice tried my best to talk him out of climbing up. Maybe they could convince him.

CHAPTER 13

TOTAL CHAOS

WE HAD NO TIME TO LOSE. WITH BIPLAB SO CLOSE to death, we descended from the summit ridge as quickly as we could. Every now and then he groaned faintly. This was good news: At least Biplab was still alive. The bad news: We'd been forced into hefting him through the peak's rocky field, and Biplab was taking a number of bruising hits. But there was no other way to transport him. We also had to worry about the elements. The temperature dropped with the sun, making the mountain even more dangerous.

Weird things stick with a person during chaotic events. I remember the perfect visibility on Kanchenjunga that day and the bright blue sky around us. Whenever I took a second to check my surroundings, or the line below, the views looked like a giant picture postcard or one of those aerial photos from *National Geographic* magazine. An hour had passed already; our route home was clearly laid out below, with Camp 4 visible in the distance. Taking into account our slow speed, I estimated we were approximately six hours away. I prayed Biplab could hold on for that long.

At around 27,560 feet (8,400 m), as I game-planned our descent, looking out hopefully for our reinforcements and those promised oxygen cylinders, I noticed another climber was slumped in the snow ahead of us. From a distance he seemed okay. His eyes were fixed on the mountains ahead. *Maybe he was taking in the scene?* But as I got closer, I recognized the same awful expression of fixed terror I'd seen in Biplab an hour or so earlier.

I shook the man's shoulder. "Hey, are you okay?"

"Yeah, I'm okay," he said, introducing himself as Kuntal, as though it were simply another afternoon on the mountain. But Kuntal's eyes wouldn't meet mine; he seemed hypnotized by the landscape. Then I registered the awful reality. *Oh no, I think he's snow-blind.*

"Why are you staying here?" I said, checking over his situation. When I looked at Kuntal's oxygen cylinder, it was empty.

"I can't get down. My guide has left me. My team left me, too." He seemed resigned to the end. His voice was eerily calm. "I think I'm gonna die."

I looked at Mingma and Gesman. *Was this really happening again?* Whatever expedition team was responsible for Kuntal had seemingly decided his climbing days were over and that he couldn't be saved.

As far as I was concerned, there was very little room for debate. On military missions I'd been encouraged to leave no operator behind. The rules were certainly different on high-altitude expeditions, but my attitude had been hardwired.

"Let's get this dude down as well," I said.

I unclipped my mask and placed it around Kuntal's face, thankful for the promise I'd made to myself after the rescue of Seema on Everest in 2016. I would always have oxygen.

Six people were attempting to escape Kanchenjunga; three were incapacitated, and the others, while being physically mobile, had given their oxygen to the ones in trouble. Our descent to Camp 4 was now going to take us a lot longer. I figured that if help didn't arrive soon, there was every chance that at least one of us would die.

> I FIGURED THAT IF HELP DIDN'T ARRIVE SOON, THERE WAS EVERY CHANCE THAT AT LEAST ONE OF US WOULD DIE.

And where were those climbers who were supposed to be helping?

I called down for assistance again. A voice told me not to worry, reassuring me that help was on the way and everything was still cool. *Was it the same person?* Through the scratch of radio interference, I couldn't be sure. But when I looked down to Camp 4 in the fading light, there was still no sign of activity. Perhaps our rescue team was gathering together in a tent to plan their mission. If so, they'd have to move fast, because our resources were dwindling at an alarming rate.

An hour after resuming our snail's pace evacuation, Gesman's strength faded. He'd already developed frostbite on his toes on Annapurna three weeks before, and his feet were prickling and tingling again, a sure sign the cold was taking another gnaw at his flesh. For one moment I became worried by his behavior, too. When I turned around to check on the group, I noticed that Gesman had yanked away Kuntal's goggles and was jabbing a finger toward his eyes.

"Brother! What's happening?"

"He's lying," shouted Gesman, furiously. "The guy can see. Look!"

He pulled a hand back, as if preparing to smack Kuntal across the face. Kuntal flinched. Then he flinched again. Apparently Gesman had noticed Kuntal reacting to one or two moments of danger. But why would a blind man hesitate before making a risky step he couldn't see? When I leaned over Kuntal and repeated the same test, he cowered with every poke and prod.

Gesman was right!

I groaned. Had Kuntal admitted the truth that he was not suffering from snow-blindness, we could have moved at a much faster pace and covered more ground. Instead, fear had caused him to lie to us. Kuntal wanted us to do the hard work for him because he'd been too scared to do it for himself. Now he was helpless and wasn't thinking straight. My temper broke. I grabbed Kuntal by the hood of his summit suit and pulled him close.

"Listen, we three are risking our lives for you, carrying you like a dead body. And you're pretending to be snow-blind. Why?"

Kuntal was too weak to answer. Despondent, Gesman grabbed him by the shoulders and lifted him up, and we continued walking into the dark, heavy shadows falling across the mountain. I didn't have the energy to waste on rage, not with the lives of so many people on the line. My anger passed.

WE FELT ABANDONED. NOBODY SEEMED TO BE COMING.

I must have radioed down to Camp 4, or Base Camp, more than a hundred times. With each communication, I became increasingly disheartened. Despite my rising frustration, I still worked hard to maintain a sense of calm, convincing myself that assistance *was* on the way. Oxygen *was* coming.

I knew at least 50 people were sleeping in the tents below. Nearly all of them had summited Kanchenjunga that same day, and it would take a rescue party only around two hours to reach our position.

Surely out of all those climbers, a small group will feel inclined to help?

With every radio call, my unease increased. Hours passed, and our situation became more and more desperate. Yet the same response was delivered over the radio every time.

"Someone is on their way to help, Nims."

"They're coming, bro."

"Not long now ..."

But from what I could tell, that someone hadn't even left Camp 4, unless they were stupid enough to climb without a headlamp. No telltale lights were approaching from below.

It was around 8 p.m. Judging by my watch, the rescue mission had taken several hours so far. The weather was fairly calm, thank god, and there was very little wind, but it was still bitterly cold. Between Gesman, Mingma, and myself, we had the skills to survive. The worrying news was that the oxygen we'd given to our rescues had run low, and due to the lack of support from below, morale was dropping.

Kuntal, withering under the stress of altitude sickness, seemed unable to communicate; Biplab was deteriorating, too. Then, not 15 minutes later, as we resumed our slow trudge to safety, I noticed something different about his body as we lowered him down, foot by foot, over the rock and ice. His pained groans had stopped; the instinctive, muscular spasms that braced against our every movement were gone.

Biplab was dead.

Desperately I checked his vitals. "Please don't let all this work have been for nothing," I sighed.

But there was no pulse; Biplab wasn't breathing. I even poked him in the eyes—the one action that usually triggered a response in a seriously injured person—but there was no reaction. When I glanced down at his oxygen cylinder, I realized the awful truth. Biplab's air had finally run out, and his body had failed.

"I'm sorry, brother; we did everything we could," I said sadly, pulling his hood down around his eyes.

I looked angrily at the lights of Camp 4. The suggestion that help was on the way had been a lie, and every request for assistance had been ignored. *But why?* I felt betrayed.

The mountain had shown me the truth about who and what I really was. On both the climb up, and the way down, I'd worked to keep our small unit alive. I could hold my head high. But a painful reality regarding some of the individuals I'd once respected within the community had also been revealed. Mountaineers who had claimed over and over that help was on the way did not come through. Instead, they slept in their tents while a man died on the line above them.

Their truth would be impossible to escape.

GESMAN LOOKED AT ME FEARFULLY. HIS FROSTBITE HAD become increasingly painful, and now it seemed he could barely walk. He had to go down. Gesman walked off into the darkness as our group said our farewells and apologies to Biplab, leaving him to the mountain. Carrying him for longer would have only slowed us down.

I figured our position would ordinarily have put us about half an hour from safety, but only if all of us were in a condition to walk fairly quickly. With only two incapacitated individuals to care for now, the journey was likely to take a painful couple of hours, maybe more, but there was no choice other than to put in the effort. Together, Mingma and I pulled and dragged Kuntal; I cajoled the guide during breaks from our heavy lifting, but Mingma was beginning to struggle, too. He was showing the first signs of altitude sickness. When we next stopped to catch our breath, I could tell something was up.

"Brother, I can't feel anything in my legs, my face, my jaw," he said. "I think I need to go down."

Mingma was the strongest Sherpa guide I'd ever known. He wasn't the type to make excuses or look for an easy way out. But he was also experienced enough to realize when his limits had been met. To push past them at that point would have meant certain death. Though I'd be alone on the mountain with a seriously injured climber and a Sherpa, I couldn't stand the thought of losing a team member to the mission.

To make matters worse, word then came through on the radio that another climber had been reported missing on the mountain. "If you see him, make sure to bring him down," crackled the voice from Base Camp. I stared angrily at the lights flickering in the distance at Camp 4. Still, nobody was moving toward us. I hugged Mingma, and then sent him on his way.

"Tell the others down there what's happening," I shouted after him.

Having been on the mountain for more than 24 hours, I was also physically destroyed, especially after those five grueling days on Dhaulagiri with barely any rest. I estimated I'd had a total of nine hours of sleep in that time. Every muscle begged me to stop. I dragged at Kuntal's weight for another two hours, the Sherpa stepping in to help from time to time, until eventually I arrived at a physical crossroad.

Option one was for me to stay with the rescue party, hoping that help and oxygen might arrive soon. But seeing as nobody had stirred from the tents below, the likeliest endgame was that we'd all die from the cold and lack of air. The second option was to leave Kuntal where he was, move quickly down to Camp 4 in about 15 minutes, then beg for a rescue party to save him. I knew that enough people would have been well rested by the time I made it down. Several climbers were certainly powerful enough to execute the mission. If I could rouse them into action, there was every chance Kuntal and the guide might be saved. I was taking option two.

"Listen, this oxygen is about to run low," I said to the Sherpa. "If Kuntal's anything like Biplab, we'll lose him soon after. But there are people in Camp 4 whom I think will listen to me. They'll come to his rescue. Either you can stay here with him or you can come with me. It's your call."

Once I'd started my descent, the Sherpa tailed me all the way down. We were confident that we could save Kuntal's life, but then a weird scene emerged in front of me. Not 50 yards (45 m) ahead we came across an old dude, wandering aimlessly around in the snow. He looked ragged. His beard was matted with ice, and he was dressed in a reflective summit suit that pinged away the light from our flashlights like laser beams.

At first, I wondered if the altitude had finally warped my thinking. No, I quickly realized that what I was seeing was the other missing climber, whom I later discovered was named Ramesh Ray, and behind him was a reassuring sight. Finally, after hours of waiting, headlamps were flickering below us in the distance. A rescue party had been mobilized. We rushed down to the lost mountaineer, holding him up until the glowing blobs became people, and the people turned into shouting voices.

"This guy needs to go down," I said as we gathered together. "You're in a better place to take him than me. And the other guy, Kuntal, is over there."

I pointed to where we'd left our casualty with a small oxygen supply. "He's not too far away. Take him some air and go and rescue him."

The mission was done. Biplab might have been lost to the mountain, but at least his guide and Kuntal would soon be safe. Hopefully the other climber was okay as well. Climbing down into camp around 1 a.m., I found Mingma's and Gesman's tent and crawled inside and pulled the sleeping bag around me for warmth. Even though I felt totally exhausted, resting was impossible. I was furious that our calls for help had been ignored. *Why were we lied to, over and over, on the radio comms?*

I could not stomach the idea of hanging around with those people. I'd find it impossible to look any of them in the eye when they awoke. I brewed tea and sat silently while Mingma and Gesman slept.

I RUMMAGED THROUGH MY BAG FOR A PAIR OF FRESH socks and packed my kit. I planned to wake Gesman and Mingma, and then descend to Base Camp, ignoring any waves from passing climbers, avoiding the gaze of anyone who approached me. But first I was going to call Suchi.

Biplab's death had broken me.

I patched a call through to England. She knew something was wrong because I rarely called her from the mountains. "Nims, what's up?" she said. I could hear the fear in her voice.

"I've failed," I said, fighting back tears. "I've failed."

I retold the story, my sadness twisting into anger. "The climbers up here were thinking only of themselves. If one of them had just brought up some air, we would have been fine. This man would have lived."

Suchi tried to soothe my distress, but I was too fired up to listen, and my mood was darkened even more after I woke Mingma and Gesman. Apparently, Rodrigo was dead, too.

At least Kuntal had been rescued and was on his way to a hospital in Kathmandu—or so I believed. While we were climbing down through Kanchenjunga's camps, a helicopter passed overhead. It was flying toward a suitable pickup point higher up the mountain, and I figured Kuntal would be on board.

I felt relieved, happy that our work hadn't been for nothing; I'd been so determined to keep everybody alive. But when I arrived at the bottom of the mountain, I was told that the chopper had only collected Ramesh Ray. From what we could decipher from the people around us, Kuntal had been left where we'd positioned him, even though the rescue party had been so close they could have reached him quite easily.

I went from feeling relieved to feeling sick. I realized the poor bloke was probably still on the mountain. There was no way he could have survived, not without oxygen. I raged at Mingma and Gesman.

"These people! They take the glory on social media, but they wouldn't do the job on the ground. They disgust me. When people needed help, where were they? I'll tell you: hiding in their tents!"

The deaths of Biplab and Kuntal felt totally unacceptable because their endings had been settled by choice. Somebody could have made an effort to help us. *They could have been saved.*

I still cannot understand why the rescue never came.

As we flew to Everest Base Camp for what would be the last three peaks in Phase One—Everest, Lhotse, and Makalu— refocusing on the job at hand became my priority. I had to muster my strength, and leave the ghosts of Kanchenjunga behind.

CHAPTER 14

EVEREST, LHOTSE, AND MAKALU

FINALLY, MY EXPEDITIONS WERE GAINING MORE attention. Additional donors wanted to invest money to help. That was good news, but I had to keep my focus.

Though Everest, Lhotse, and Makalu felt like home territory because of my world-record climb the previous year, none of them were to be taken lightly. Every Death Zone mountain posed a challenge.

As I readied myself for the final three mountains of Phase One, I realized Project Possible now presented me with the platform to speak out on climate change, something I'd hoped to do when I first announced my idea. People were watching my progress. I needed to talk about how climate change was affecting the mountains and the rest of the world. I posted one or two comments on social media, each one outlining my thoughts.

I'd climbed my first mountain in 2012. Just seven years later, I was on my way to climbing all 14 Death Zones peaks in seven months. I'd proven to everybody that with a positive attitude and self-confidence, it was never too late to follow your dreams and make them come true. If I could pull off such a feat with climbing, what could we do together to make positive environmental change around the world? As people responded to my comments on climate change, I felt motivated to do more.

Some of the people I was interacting with online were kids, teenagers, and young adults on the verge of making their first big life decisions, such as who to vote for or what career choices to make. Some of them were considering their first mountain climb. They were the type of people emotionally invested in the future of the Himalaya and the environment. I wanted to show them exactly what was happening to the world at high altitude, the good and the bad.

I'd already decided that my efforts should begin close to home. I insisted that our missions be as environmentally friendly as possible. I was the expedition leader, so I had it in my power to instigate change. Everything we took to the mountain, we brought back down with us. We weren't leaving trash on the mountains, and I required those I took on climbs to do the same. I always made my position clear.

"Yeah, you come here for the love of nature, but if you don't respect it, you've got no place in my expedition," I told them. "If you don't follow the rules, you can take your money and you can leave." Most people on my climbs turned up with a passion for the environment, so getting them to follow my rules wasn't hard.

I realized that the best way to draw attention to climate change through Project Possible was to shout about it from the mountaintops.

I REALLY WANTED TO BREAK MY SPEED WORLD RECORD for climbing Everest, Lhotse, and Makalu. In 2017, I'd gone from the peak of Everest to Lhotse in 10 hours and 15 minutes. By the end of my trip with the G200E team, I had climbed all three mountains in five days. On my way to Everest Base Camp for the Project Possible expedition, I decided that it was probably within my reach to cut that time by half. I believed in my mental and physical strength. Those mountains were beasts, but I'd become fairly familiar with them. Still, I knew to respect their dangers.

We began our Everest climb on May 22, 2019, a little later than other expeditions that year. For this climb I was accompanied by Lakpa Dendi, one of the guides who had helped out the Gurkhas during the G200E expedition in 2017. As we moved up the mountain, dawn was cracking in the sky above us. I noticed the flash of cameras going off and the flicker of headlamps ahead. A few groups were in front of us, and they were moving slowly, tired from the effort of having climbed so far. We soon stepped past them to hit the summit. It took us three hours to reach the summit from Camp 4. Even though I had seen this view before, it was just as incredible this time.

The morning sun was rising above the Himalaya. As one or two other climbers joined us at the top, everybody seemed energized. The guys who had looked spent on the line up only moments earlier were immediately full of life. It was as if the new sun had delivered us all a fresh burst of purpose and optimism, even in the freezing cold. *If only I could soak up the light all day.* Then I felt somebody tugging at my summit suit. It was Lakpa.

"Brother, we should go," he said. "If you want to break that record, we need to turn around now."

I nodded, grabbing a few photographs before stepping off the peak. Soon after turning around, I was greeted with a chaotic scene. A long line was snaking around the ridge leading to the summit. There were probably about 150 climbers squeezed onto the fixed line, with people moving slowly in both directions. We tried to edge down the rope carefully, checking in with each person we passed, but I sensed in many of them a growing mood of panic.

Some people, I could see, were angry. They had invested a lot of money, time, and effort to scale Everest, and their progress had been stopped, like traffic on a highway, as climbers moved in opposite directions. I feared that some of them were taking serious risks with their lives and the safety of those around them by not descending before their oxygen became too low.

It was fast becoming a dangerous situation. I overheard one person complaining that his toes and fingers were starting to become frostbitten. Anyone moving along this ridge was presented with dangers on either side: There was a 7,874-foot (2,400-m) drop to the left and a 9,842-foot (3,000-m) drop to the right. A climber falling from that height wasn't coming back.

The people I worried about the most were those climbers lost in the chaos; they were in fear and emotionally spiraling. Anxiety at high altitude isn't too different from a drowning event. In the middle of the ocean, someone who thinks they're about to go under will grab at anything or anyone to stay afloat. They thrash and panic, often yanking the nearest person down with them in a desperate attempt to survive. The same thing can happen high up.

With summit fever and anxiety growing among the different groups, I felt the emotional temperature on Everest was approaching a boiling point. People were arguing around me; somebody was about to act recklessly. Because several lives had been lost on Everest already that year, I recognized something drastic needed to happen in order to keep people safe.

I climbed to a small rock ledge that overlooked the queue. The scene below me was ugly. Both lanes of traffic had claimed the right of way, and neither side wanted to move. Collisions were taking place every couple of minutes, which threatened to wobble somebody from the safety rope at any moment.

I noticed a Sherpa, conscious of the craziness, begging his clients to turn around, fearful for their lives. Some agreed reluctantly. Others ignored him. Everything was madness. With nobody else stepping up to help, I started organizing the congestion.

At first, I ushered through the climbers who had been waiting the longest. In many ways, my role wasn't that different from a police officer directing traffic. Instead of cars, I was waving through mountaineers. Some of them were so fatigued, they seemed to have forgotten the basic skills required for high-altitude climbing. Altitude sickness had gripped them. I checked in with the Sherpas who were guiding clients who were visibly struggling. If I sensed it wasn't safe for them to try to continue, I suggested the guides should send them down.

In the end, I remained for close to two hours. With every assessment, I knew any chance of breaking my own world record was diminishing. Once the logjam had cleared, around 90 percent of the crowd had either summited with enough time to turn around, or were winding their way down to Camp 4. It was time for me to make the same move. Heading to Lhotse was now my main goal.

If I wanted to break my world record for climbing Everest and Lhotse, I estimated I was at least three hours behind schedule. I wasn't too concerned. If I could shave an hour or so off my previous time, I'd still fulfill my goal, though I would undoubtedly be tired.

Lhotse was a steep incline. Pulling myself along the fixed line was a challenge. For long periods my quads and calves burned as I put one foot in front of the other. To prevent my muscles from burning out, I switched techniques, sidestepping up the mountain, like a crab.

The climb across Lhotse was surrounded by both beauty and brutality. Ahead was the massive presence of Everest, standing tall, dressed in clouds. I could still see a line of people descending toward Camp 4.

I topped Lhotse with a time of 10 hours and 15 minutes, matching my time from 2017, but there was still plenty of hard work to be done.

I was able to climb Makalu quickly, too. I helicoptered to Base Camp and rested up for a few hours before moving to the peak with Geljen. The lines had been fixed, the snow covering was shallow, and we moved fast and light, reaching the summit in 18 hours on May 24, 2019.

Phase One of the mission had been completed. I'd broken one of the two world records I was going for. I'd climbed from the summit of Everest to the summits of Lhotse and then Makalu in 48 hours and 30 minutes, smashing my time from 2017.

The holdup on Everest had stopped me from bettering my time from the summit of Everest to the summit of Lhotse, but I had bigger things to focus on. It was time to move to Phase Two.

CHAPTER 15

ENTERING PHASE TWO

MOM WASN'T GETTING ANY BETTER. IN FACT, HER heart condition was worsening.

While she rested in the hospital in Kathmandu, Binesh, a close family friend, gave her regular updates on Project Possible. When I'd moved through the Himalaya in May 2019, Binesh sat by her bed, reading her newspaper stories about my expeditions and world records. He showed her video clips from Facebook and explained how I'd made some rescues. When I got to Kathmandu after finishing Phase One, I visited her in the hospital as much as I could, holding her hand while I retold my stories. After a while, she looked at me and smiled. "It sounds like my son is unstoppable," she said.

Mom knew how important Project Possible was to me, and she'd come to accept my passion, even though some of the risks I'd been taking clearly worried her. Mom also knew that I was going to do everything in my power to get her and Dad into an apartment together, once my work was done. Seeing her in a hospital bed attached to wires and beeping machines was very upsetting. Tears streaked her cheeks as we spoke. My mom was everything to me. She'd made me the man I was, and I hated the thought of leaving her behind. There was a moment of doubt.

Mom seemed to sense I was worried. "Nims, you've started this mission now," she said. "So complete it. Our blessings are with you."

> MY MOM WAS EVERYTHING TO ME. SHE'D MADE ME THE MAN I WAS, AND I HATED THE THOUGHT OF LEAVING HER BEHIND.

I squeezed her hand and promised to return home safely again as soon as I could.

Quitting was not in our blood.

I MOVED INTO PHASE TWO OF PROJECT POSSIBLE AT THE end of June 2019. It would take me to Nanga Parbat, Gasherbrum I and II, K2, and Broad Peak in Pakistan. The conversation surrounding my goals within the extreme mountaineering community had shifted to be a bit more positive, but only slightly. Yes, a number of people were impressed by the speed at which I'd climbed all six mountains in the first chunk of the mission, but there were plenty of others who still doubted me. I just kept moving forward.

I understood that the mountains in Pakistan presented different challenges from those in Nepal. It was a more unpredictable region in which to climb. The weather was known for being vicious on K2, the second highest mountain in the world. Across Gasherbrum I and II, huge storms could blow in out of nowhere, bringing whiteout conditions on an otherwise sunny day. The support at base camps in this region, such as communications and accommodation, was also less sophisticated than in Nepal. I would have to trek between base camps rather than taking a helicopter.

My biggest stress when climbing in Pakistan, though, was the threat of my team being wiped out in a terrorist attack on Nanga Parbat. An attack from Taliban forces was a very real concern during the months building up to Project Possible. It had happened in 2013, and the threat remained.

Taliban fighters could arrive quickly, because it took only a day to trek to the region where Nanga Parbat was located. Taliban forces made my getting to K2 and Gasherbrum I and II risky as well. I would have to pass through a number of military checkpoints. I would be unarmed and unable to defend myself if life got noisy as we waited at Base Camp. I also had several others on the team to consider, and none of them had any military experience.

The other concern was that my mission had gained more and more attention over the months. This made me a high-level target for terrorists looking to make a name for themselves. My background in the military was hardly a secret, and anyone with an axe to grind about my involvement in the War on Terror would find me exposed and vulnerable on Nanga Parbat. *I would have to work carefully.*

CHAPTER 16

NANGA PARBAT

DID EVERYTHING I COULD TO KEEP THE NANGA PARBAT climb safe.

To confuse any potential terrorists, I booked three different flights into Pakistan throughout July, hoping to cover my tracks. I didn't publicize any of my movements on social media until I'd made it away in one piece.

As a final precaution, I separated myself from our private client, an accomplished mountaineer who had paid to top Nanga Parbat alongside the team. I decided it was probably safer if she met up with us at Base Camp.

Even my teammates were forced into a procedural change or two, which included an adjustment to our relaxed attitude in the mountains. We would have to be on alert at all times. We had to operate quickly and quietly.

When a van arrived to take us from Islamabad, Pakistan, toward Nanga Parbat, the driver's radio was playing. We allowed ourselves a bit of a celebration before reaching the mountain. We turned the volume up, singing and shouting as we started our journey into the mountains. I soon got a reminder of how careful we'd have to be. A call came from Muhammad Ali Sadpara, a renowned mountaineer.

Ali had climbed Nanga Parbat a number of times already. He knew the area well, and I'd asked him to be our base camp manager. Hearing the music and singing in the background as we spoke, Ali reminded me of our need to be unseen and unheard during the coming week.

"This is not Nepal. No messing around!" There was no room for error, not even loud music on the road.

His warning freaked me out a little bit, but he was right. It was a reminder I felt I should not have needed. When we started our trek to Nanga Parbat, the team trudged silently at night through villages and past trekking lodges. We remained focused. Once we got to Base Camp, I drew upon the defensive skills learned in my military training. As the sun went down, I remained alert, checking in at each tent. The guys were chatting quietly.

Every now and then I'd watch the horizon for approaching lights, or signs of any unusual activity, but watching for danger was only half the battle. I knew our position could be compromised by a tweet or Instagram post from one of the other expedition parties waiting at Nanga Parbat, so I called together their team leaders, asking them to be discreet about our location and not to tag me or our team on social media. I couldn't take the risk that a terrorist group in Pakistan might pick up on a photo or other information and come for us. Plus, it wouldn't just put our team in danger, but everyone else in the area would be put at risk, too.

I was erring on the side of caution, and I knew it was the right thing to do.

A FEW EXPEDITION PARTIES HAD ARRIVED IN NANGA
Parbat before us, including climbers from Jordan, Russia, France,
and Italy. We found out from them that lines were fixed and
securely in place from Camp 2 to Camp 3. An international team
had fixed the lines from Camp 1 to Camp 2. Our team planned
accordingly. Since we wouldn't have to fix any lines early on, we
could carry equipment on our way up.

As soon as we were settled, I led a rotation from Base Camp
toward Camp 1 to acclimate to the altitude. Soon after we started
our ascent, a heavy weather system closed in around us. The
mountain was blanketed by a snowstorm. Our luck worsened
once we pushed past Camp 1. The lines set by the international
team were nowhere to be found.

The fear that the line had not been fully secured started to
nag at me. I hoped the lines might have just been covered by the
snow. We dug furiously through the growing snowdrifts. It was a
lot of work. Meanwhile, the terrain around us was so steep that
the snow above us had the
potential to unload and rush
through the rocks like a
heavy white lava flow.

**A HUGE SWELL OF POWDER
WAS POURING IN FROM
OVERHEAD, SOON SMASHING
EVERYBODY SIDEWAYS.**

Then it happened. I rec-
ognized an all-too-familiar
whooshing sound. A huge swell of powder was pouring in from
overhead, soon smashing everybody sideways. At the time, I'd
had my eyes on Mingma. He was reaching around for some sign
of a buried rope. The white swallowed him up in an instant.

I panicked. *Was I about to lose him?*

Gathering my senses, I crawled through the billowing fog and powder around us, hoping for some indication that Mingma had survived until, thankfully, he came into view. He had saved himself from a fatal drop off a nearby ledge by forcing his arms into the drifts around him, but his position was dangerous. In the chaos, his legs had twisted, and his grip on the snow was barely strong enough to hold his weight in place. One wrong move might collapse the snow around him and release him.

> ONE WRONG MOVE MIGHT COLLAPSE THE SNOW AROUND HIM AND RELEASE HIM.

Slowly we worked our way toward Mingma. By fixing a couple of ice axes into the snow as makeshift handholds, we were able to give him a firm grip, and he untangled his limbs before climbing his way to safety. A fatal crisis had been averted.

I'd had enough of looking for the lines. They weren't there, so we descended to Base Camp. I was determined to confront the international crew. They had lied about the lines and put us in grave danger. I was also annoyed with myself. I'd been too trusting.

I found some of the international climbers, and my anger at their fake lines and Mingma's near-death experience intensified. I stormed into their tent.

"Why did you lie?" I shouted. "Why did you say you'd fixed the lines when you hadn't? I nearly lost my most capable guy because of you."

To my surprise, they made no attempt to talk their way out of it.

"Nims, we're sorry," said one in the group. "The lines are *partly* fixed. We put the word up on Twitter, but maybe it wasn't detailed enough. We didn't expect you guys to be looking at it, too."

"Yeah, but it caused me to plan differently. I'd have gone light rather than carrying a super-heavy load."

At that point I realized that the only trustworthy people on Nanga Parbat were the guys from Project Possible. I also understood our summit push wasn't going to be made any easier if I was upset with everyone else in Base Camp.

I checked myself; it was the right moment to simmer down. "Listen, brothers, we have to be honest with each other," I said, lowering my voice. "From now on we'll only deal with accurate information. To climb this mountain, we need to have a solid plan."

I suggested the line-fixing workload should be shared between the different teams during our summit push. We agreed and made a plan. We were scheduled to head up for the summit the following week, on July 3, 2019. The weather was supposed to be better by then.

When the climbing began for real, the Project Possible team trailblazed across the mountain toward Camp 2, digging out any submerged rope before resting in our tents for the night. We were thankful for at least some sleep. The Jordanian team proved to be a powerful group and unafraid of sharing the heavy workload. They led the way to Camp 3 the following morning.

As we climbed, we heard some bickering among the other teams. Though we weren't directly involved, the squabbling was distracting. My team kept our focus and moved forward.

My frustrations with the other teams turned up a notch the morning after we'd stayed overnight at Camp 3 and trailblazed across a steep incline to Camp 4, where the snow was deep and the line-fixing effort was physically intense. To prepare for our summit push, the expedition parties decided to rest at Camp 4 for a few hours, though there was very little chance to sleep. Six people were crammed into one tent because we'd decided to travel across the mountain with as few supplies as possible.

When it was time to depart, the other teams had gathered together and were waiting for us to lead yet again. I was annoyed, but we kept going.

When I looked down from the slope—we were climbing on our summit push—the exposure was intense and Base Camp was visible through the clouds. My heart pounded. My hands felt sweaty. As a group we decided to sidestep across the icy incline. One misstep might cause me to hurtle past the other teams climbing beneath me and land on the rock below. I looked at the others; they seemed to be moving fairly steadily. Then I called out to Geljen. He had taken on most of the trailblazing between Camps 3 and 4. When we had awakened for the summit push that morning, he had looked pale. The effort had been that intense. Now, he seemed almost broken.

Surely he was feeling the fear, too?

"Hey bro, is this not a bit sketchy?" I shouted.

Geljen laughed. "Yeah! It's crazy, Nimsdai. Let's be super careful."

Knowing it wasn't just me, I gave a sigh of relief. But that one tingle of fear caused me to reevaluate our situation. I had to refocus. I began kicking my crampons into the mountain. The metal teeth were shredding chunks of ice away to form a deep foothold. I then gouged out another with my ice axe. And another.

"Guys, kick out a path for the others!" I shouted. "Otherwise, someone might take a lethal fall up here."

We carved our way to the very top, while digging out a visible trail for the others. The team eventually made it to the summit of Nanga Parbat around 10 a.m. on July 3, 2019. Teamwork and shared focus had pushed Project Possible to the top of our first Pakistani peak.

LEAVING THE SUMMIT OF NANGA PARBAT, I'D BEEN EAGER to get to Base Camp. We rested overnight at Camp 4 before descending early in the morning. Having moved into the soft powder that had nearly sucked in Mingma a few days earlier, I stepped down carefully, holding the line on a steep slope. It was steep enough that I should have been even more careful.

Why I became distracted, I don't know. When a climber from below shouted that I should get off the line, I unclipped myself, stepped back, and continued down without thinking. I guess he hadn't wanted any extra tension on the rope, which was unreasonable, but I was happy to give way, as it seemed he was having some trouble. This was a near-fatal move on my part.

When unclipping from the line and stepping back, I relaxed for just a moment and lost my full focus. It was a sloppy move. I skidded backward, landing on my back and banging my head before spinning and sliding down the mountain, faster and faster. Yard after yard rushed by in a blur.

I yanked at the leash holding my ice axe in place. I shoved my pick into the snow, hoping it would slow my speed. If I could only stop my fall, I could walk back to the rope. But the axe wouldn't hold. I stabbed at the snow with my axe again and again, but the surface was too fluffy for it to hold.

Now was the time not to panic. *I was in a free fall.* I spotted the rope alongside me. If I could just grab that, I'd have a fighting chance of survival. Reaching out, I grabbed hard. I pulled myself to a stop. Somehow, miraculously, I hadn't been killed.

As I clipped myself back onto the line, my legs wobbling a little, I made a promise to myself. *I'll always concentrate; I'll always get down safely.* I crept down the mountain slowly, repeating the words over and over.

There was no time for celebration. We left Nanga Parbat and headed for our next challenge. I had rarely felt so lucky to be alive.

CHAPTER 17

GASHERBRUM I AND II

ROJECT POSSIBLE WAS TEACHING ME LESSON AFTER lesson, on and off the mountain. At sea level, I was developing my skills as a fundraiser, a one-man PR machine, an environmental campaigner, and a political mover. Above 26,000 feet (8,000 m), I'd learned more about my true capabilities under pressure, that I could lead and stay calm while managing potential disasters, such as severe altitude sickness, avalanches, and rescue operations. When presented with near-death situations, such as my fall on Nanga Parbat, I faced the danger head on, thinking and acting fast. There was no other way to survive.

Gasherbrum I (GI) and Gasherbrum II (GII), the 11th and 13th highest mountains in the world, were the next peaks on the Phase Two schedule. There was no time to waste.

The journey from Nanga Parbat to the town of Skardu and then on to the shared Base Camp of GI and GII was supposed to take eight days. We were set to travel through a couple of areas known to be patrolled by Taliban fighters. It was important that everybody remain on high alert until we reached the Karakoram mountain range. Taking extra precaution to stay out of sight, we also camped away from the trekking lodges on the road.

We drove nonstop for 24 hours for the first part of the journey, the entire team and our supplies jammed into a minivan. When a landslide on the road threatened to slow us down, we unloaded our backpacks and equipment. Then we loaded them into another vehicle on the other side of the slide. I knew that resting unnecessarily when a hostile force was nearby would be way too dangerous.

We finally arrived in the town of Askole, the starting point for most treks throughout the Karakoram region. Before the walking phase of our journey began, we hired mules and porters to carry most of our equipment the rest of the way, but I worried they might move too slowly along the trails and hold us back. Before we set off, I asked the porters to double the number of mules. I figured that with lighter loads, they could go faster. Time was against us, as mountaineering season was coming to a close. Plus, I had decided that I didn't merely want to break the world record of two years for climbing the region's five mountains that are higher than 26,000 feet (8,000 m). I wanted to destroy it.

THERE WAS A FIRE IN MY BELLY, BUT MY TEAM WAS BEING HELD BACK.

There was a fire in my belly, but my team was being held back.

"Look, we can't go at the normal speed," I said to the lead porter. "If we can get to GI in three days, instead of the eight it usually takes, I'll still pay you for the full eight."

The porter wasn't having it. "Nims, it doesn't matter whether the mules carry sixty-five pounds or ninety pounds. They always travel at the same speed."

The following morning, as we were about to depart from Askole, the porter arrived with the same number of mules. He was adamant that reinforcements weren't useful. On the first night, we waited for four or five hours for our porters to catch up with us as we camped. The same thing happened the following evening. On the third, I became impatient. We needed to move faster.

I checked in with Mingma, Geljen, Gesman, and the rest of our team. "If we can carry our climbing kit by ourselves, we'll be so much quicker. Are you willing?"

The team nodded, everyone in agreement. We left our camp at 4 a.m. and arrived at the bottom of GI around 5 p.m., covering 34 miles (54 km) in 13 hours. We each carried a lot more than usual, and we were exhausted.

Despite the huge effort it had taken to get there, I felt ready for this stretch of the mission, confident we could tackle the challenges ahead, but respectful of what I was about to take on. GI wasn't as harsh as K2 or Annapurna, but it was still an intense mountain. It wasn't to be taken lightly, especially after I'd nearly wiped out on Nanga Parbat.

I often acknowledged that the odds I might die were quite high during an expedition, and there was always a chance that I could seriously hurt myself, but that's as far as I ever went. I never contemplated how it might happen or the pain I might experience. Instead, I focused on my reputation as an expert mountaineer. I recalled the importance of being brave and acting with integrity. Strength and smarts could take me anywhere. I would prevail.

Having settled in at GI and GII's shared Base Camp, I focused on how to overcome any traps the mountains might have laid.

I put aside bad thoughts regarding my fall on Nanga Parbat, and began another dialogue with the mountains.

So, come on then. This is you versus me.

This is yours, Nims. This is where you come alive.

My mindset before any climb was neither fearful nor overly relaxed. My aim was always to be aggressive. *Whenever I attack a mountain, I attack at 100 percent.*

I knew more than anyone that nature didn't care for reputation, age, gender, or background. It didn't discriminate. All I could do was to put myself in the right frame of mind, and never lose my focus.

Deep snow? *I will trailblaze like a hundred men.*

Avalanches? *I can mitigate.*

Crazy whiteouts? *Bring 'em on.*

I needed to make myself a solid force on every mountain, capable of smashing through any obstacle. Then it was go time.

WE SET A BATTLE PLAN WHILE WE RESTED AT BASE CAMP. GII posed the smaller challenge, and we intended to take it at a relatively leisurely pace, resting in some of the lower camps as we climbed. GI was the bigger test, so I wanted to climb it first along with Mingma and Geljen.

The work was grueling. Nobody had dropped any air off for us in advance, so the team needed to load up with oxygen cylinders, a full mountain kit, equipment, and supplies. After starting the climb, even after two days of rest, it didn't take long to figure out we were still tired after our journey from Nanga Parbat. As we moved forward, our energy levels dropped quickly.

Thankfully, fixed lines would take us all the way up, and I was fairly hopeful we could climb GI in pretty good time.

I'd previously topped Makalu, the world's fifth highest mountain, in 18 hours after climbing through Everest and Lhotse while barely sleeping for four or five days. I'd scaled Kanchenjunga, the world's third highest mountain, in similar circumstances, after having come through a rough expedition on Dhaulagiri. I figured we had it in us to do the northwest face of Gasherbrum I, at 26,509 feet (8,080 m), in one push. By my estimate, we'd reach the summit around midday.

One of the biggest challenges was a steep, 70-degree ridge that divided Camp 2 from the higher camps. Once we'd climbed above it, our job was to pull ourselves to the top, the final stages involving a traverse across another sharp incline. The work was tough; it took us much longer than expected, and by the time we reached Camp 3, the sun had set. There was no way to press on. We had to rethink our plans.

I knew that forging ahead in the dark would be too risky. We weren't entirely sure of where the summit was. There wasn't a route marker in sight, and we would almost certainly become disoriented when figuring out the exact route up, even with our GPS.

The more pressing issue was our lack of equipment. Because the plan had been to push toward the summit in one go and we'd failed, our operation now felt vulnerable. In order to complete the expedition in time, we'd need to stay at Camp 3, where there was an old broken tent for us to crawl into. Once in the shelter, we could rest for a few hours until the time came for our summit push in the morning. But the team had traveled light. We had only oxygen cylinders with us. There was no food and we had only our summit suits for warmth, plus one sleeping bag.

Our only option to stay warm was to huddle together. Our body heat saved us from plummeting temperatures. At 3 a.m., too cold to sleep, we got ready for the summit push. It took 90 minutes for everyone to get their stuff together. We were exhausted.

> OUR ONLY OPTION TO STAY WARM WAS TO HUDDLE TOGETHER. OUR BODY HEAT SAVED US FROM PLUMMETING TEMPERATURES.

The climb to the top was a slog. We moved up the slope without ropes, confused as to which way to turn in the early morning light. *Was the peak to the left or the right?* I couldn't tell, but I had to know for sure that we were heading in the right direction. There were too many horror stories of climbers scaling one summit, only to be told they'd reached a false peak after making it back to Base Camp. I didn't want to suffer as a result of a navigational error, and exhaustion was threatening to overwhelm me with every step. I called down to Base Camp and was patched through to a climber who had made it to the top a couple of weeks before.

Following his directions, we found our way to the GI summit on July 15. We took a moment to take in the sight of GII and the Broad Peak mountains in the distance.

Nature at that altitude could be both beautiful and violent. Beholding the Himalaya stretching out before me on GI somehow jolted me back to my first ever moment on Everest's summit. I remembered standing there with Pasang, feeling relief at first. I'd overcome a scary brush with high-altitude pulmonary edema, and my fingers and toes seemed close to snapping in the cold, but the first glimmer of sunlight through the peaks had changed everything. Everest's energy shifted from dark to light, death to life, and I knew I'd make it home.

That same feeling was happening on GI. Our struggles felt distant, from another lifetime. Especially now, with the mountaintops glowing, the clouds around them burning away, I felt a new day was kicking off.

My calm state left me as soon we turned around for our descent. I looked down. The ground seemed to rush up at me as the memory of my tumble on Nanga Parbat flashed back for a split second. Without a safety line, I suddenly felt vulnerable and very exposed. I watched nervously as Geljen and Mingma turned around and began digging their ice axes into the slope, stepping down backward, as though it were just another routine descent. *But was it?* I wasn't so sure. My legs were wobbling, my adrenaline was racing, and for the first time in the mission I feared for my life. Self-doubt hit hard.

It would be quite easy to slip here. *Would I die?*

We weren't tethered together. *Why didn't I bring any rope?*

If I lost my balance, I'd go into free fall.

These emotions were a shock, but I'd been vulnerable because I'd forgotten one of my most important rules: Do not underestimate a mountain. I had underestimated this one. Another unfamiliar reality was even scarier: I didn't feel confident. I turned around and drove my crampons into the ice, moving down slowly, cautiously, step-by-step, my heart banging through my chest. Once we made it to flatter ground, I felt more at ease and walked confidently to Camp 3. I prayed this feeling would pass.

I needed to dust myself off and get back in the game.

AS WE MOVED DOWN TO CAMP 2, I CHECKED IN WITH BASE Camp, and a message from another expedition pinged my satellite phone.

"Nimsdai! There's a climber called Mathias stuck at Camp 2. Can you call out to him and bring him down?"

It was around 3 p.m. Knowing that we were fairly close to Mathias, we saw no reason not to help. We found him and waited as he gathered his stuff together. Five minutes passed. Then 10. At one point, Mathias announced that he would be ready in "just a few." Geljen pressed on to the next camp, assuming that we'd catch up with him fairly quickly. Once 15 minutes had slipped by, we were thankfully on the move again. I was freezing cold and exhausted. The delay had cost us.

From nowhere, a heavy weather system swept in and within minutes we were swaddled in clouds as the heavens dumped a blanket of snow on us. Our visibility was reduced to nothing, and in the confusion I heard a cry. *Mingma!* He'd taken a misstep and been sucked into an unseen crevasse. I crawled across to find him but was careful not to plunge into another hidden break. I feared the worst. When I peered into the body-size hole, Mingma was peering back at me. By some sheer fluke, his bag had snagged on the edge, fixing his body in place. With some careful wriggling, Mingma was able to free his arms and grab hold on the ice as we lifted him out. That was two near-death scrapes he'd endured in as many mountains.

After rescuing Mingma, I had a thought: *If Mingma could slip into an unseen crevasse, would Geljen be okay?* Without a clear view to Camp 1 through the clouds, there was every chance he might step away from the line and disappear into the mountain as Mingma had. I grabbed my radio and attempted to call him back, but there was no answer. Then I heard a faint beep and a crackle of static in my backpack. Oh, no. *Geljen had left his comms behind!*

I took a quick moment to check on our situation. There was no way up; the route was shrouded in mist. We didn't have much of a chance climbing down either. The snow was too heavy to see through. At first, the three of us set about digging a hole into the snow with our ice axes. If we could create enough of a breaker from the growing wind and whiteout conditions, there was hope that we might stay warm enough by cuddling tightly. But as we hacked and chipped away, there didn't seem to be enough room to protect us all. I knew that if we hung around for too much longer, we might die. The time had come to take an even riskier step.

I KNEW THAT IF WE HUNG AROUND FOR TOO MUCH LONGER, WE MIGHT DIE. THE TIME HAD COME TO TAKE AN EVEN RISKIER STEP.

"We're going to have to get back up to Camp 2," I said.

I looked at Mathias. "Is there enough room for us to get into your tent up there?"

He nodded. We'd been presented with a shot of survival at least, but it was a risky one. If Mingma's experience was anything to go by, there was a good chance one of us might fall into another crevasse. Cautiously, we moved back up to Camp 2. Every now and then I'd radio down to the expeditions below, hopeful that Geljen might have made it down to Camp 1, but nobody had seen him.

Was Geljen still alive?

I was beginning to fear the worst. It was only once we'd made it through the cloud and squeezed into a small two-man tent for shelter that I felt safe. Then my radio beeped and coughed with static.

"Nimsdai! I'm home!"

It was Geljen. He was in one piece and had borrowed a radio from another climber. For a brief moment, we had room to breathe.

WE MADE IT THROUGH THE NIGHT, SHIVERING IN freezing conditions for several hours. As we climbed down the next morning, my confidence gradually returned. I felt stronger and more comfortable dealing with extreme exposure. By the time we made it back to Base Camp, the worst of the wobbles I'd experienced at the top of GI were behind me, or so I hoped. My plan was to work hard on managing my emotions through GII, because I would need every ounce of resilience to survive the even more challenging terrain of K2. For now, I focused on the primary mission by leaning into an age-old military saying: "Prepare for the worst; hope for the best."

When I looked up at GII from Camp 1, a peak that was considered to be fairly calm, I readied myself for a challenge. We weren't planning on climbing all 26,358 feet (8,034 m) of it in one go. Instead, the team would rest at Camps 2 and 3.

As we worked our way up the mountain, GII was calm. We summited on July 18, 2019, and I felt awe and excitement. In the distance was K2. It looked beautiful. The sharp peak curved toward the skyline like a shark's tooth; it was glowing pink in the sunrise.

I'm going to be on top of that. And I'm going to show the world how it's done.

CHAPTER 18

K2

NOT EVERYONE SHARED MY OPTIMISM. AS WE MADE our way down GII, I learned that the weather on K2 had been pretty bad. A number of experienced climbers were waiting at Base Camp, and several expedition parties were holding out there for a better weather window. Some of them had been hanging around for months. Around 200 climbing permits had been issued by the Pakistani authorities that year, but about 95 percent of those hoping to climb K2 had packed up and gone home.

I passed several teams that were trekking away from the mountain as I arrived, many of them stopping to tell us their K2 horror stories. There had been at least two summit attempts, but on both occasions, the line-fixing teams brave enough to attack the peak had been beaten back by horrendous conditions. They had made it only past Camp 4 and onto a section called the Bottleneck, a thin area below the peak at 26,903 feet (8,200 m). Meanwhile, a number of ridges along the way were ready to explode with avalanches. Even the Sherpas were in fear of what might happen up there.

When we joined the others at Base Camp, I was pulled aside by Mingma Sherpa, a friend of mine with serious expertise on the big mountains. He had set the lines on K2 twice in recent years and was regarded as an excellent climber within the guiding community. This time, though, the mountain had spooked him.

"Nimsdai, it's so, *so* dangerous to climb," he said, pulling out his phone to play several minutes of video footage captured from his attempt at the summit a few days earlier. "Take a look."

The snow was chest-deep in some sections, which wasn't going to be a physical issue for me, or my team, but every step was loaded with risk. At one point, according to Mingma Sherpa, the lead climber in the fixing team had been swept away by an avalanche. Luckily, Mingma Sherpa had survived, but the video certainly had me worried.

I gathered my team around me. It was time to prepare for the worst.

MY MISSION WAS IN JEOPARDY.

As I met with the various expedition parties at Base Camp and figured out how best to tackle K2, an update arrived regarding my permit request for Shishapangma—the world's 14th highest mountain and the final peak on our schedule. Located in Tibet, it was up to the Chinese government to decide who could climb it and who couldn't. For the entire 2019 mountaineering season, it had been decided that nobody would be granted access to the peak.

K2

I'd hoped that they might make an exception, given the scale of my mission, but the news wasn't great. The Chinese Mountaineering Association had turned me down citing a number of safety concerns, and Shishapangma was to remain closed— no exceptions. The chances of my climbing the final mountain of Phase Three seemed increasingly unlikely.

It was hard not to feel a little disheartened. So far, I had scaled every peak on the schedule in the time and style I had planned. The team had proven self-sufficient and effective, and we'd worked with speed. This news was disappointing, but I wasn't going to let it derail me. There would be some way of finishing the job. *There had to be.* For now, the focus was on K2.

So far, my tactic for the big peaks had been to lead experienced Nepali climbers to the top of mountains they had yet to scale. But I also had to consider how best to tackle K2. Before showing up at Base Camp, I'd been toying with the idea of taking on Broad Peak first. A small expedition party had climbed it a few days earlier, and all the trailblazing and line-fixing had been completed. But when I spoke to the other climbers at K2, I realized they'd been waiting for me to arrive. They wanted to see if my team could finish the rope-fixing job. My success or failure would determine whether they continued, or packed up and went home. That increased the pressure on us for sure, but I liked the idea of helping those climbers reach their dream of scaling one of the most dangerous peaks on Earth.

I needed all the experience and manpower I could get. On K2, the weather continued to be really bad, and high winds were

> MY SUCCESS OR FAILURE WOULD DETERMINE WHETHER THEY CONTINUED, OR PACKED UP AND WENT HOME.

predicted for the next few days. It would be painfully cold, too. I understood that failure on K2 would mean I'd have to make a second attempt at it before climbing Broad Peak, and by that point the Pakistan climbing season would be over.

Time was tight, and I planned accordingly. It was up to us to fix the last of the lines on the mountain above Camp 4. I hoped to climb K2 with Gesman and Lakpa Dendi Sherpa. The mountain's unforgiving nature and the sketchy conditions around the peak required a plan with military precision.

"We know this is a risky climb," I said. "The work is going to be rough. My plan is to assess the situation from Camp 4. Gesman and Lakpa Dendi, you're coming with me. If it's too dangerous up there, we'll come down, and I'll swap you out. Mingma and Geljen, you'll then fall in behind and we'll go again. I'm going to rotate two guys every time so you can rest, but I'm going to lead this thing from the front. And I'm only giving up when we've made at least six, seven attempts at the top."

There was another pressing issue to deal with, too. Many of the climbers waiting nervously at Base Camp were rattled by fear, and some of them appeared to be beaten already. They felt unnerved when they learned that other big-time mountaineers were unable to scale K2,. A number of individuals even wanted to bail out and go home. Several people were freaked out, having watched a line-fixer be swept away by an avalanche ahead of them.

One afternoon, Clara, a woman from the Czech Republic whom I'd known to be a very strong climber, came to my tent. She was scared.

"Look, Nims, I don't think I can do this. It's too much."

The morale at Base Camp was broken. It was up to me to fix

it. When I gathered everybody together for a group briefing, I outlined my plan, telling the expedition parties how I intended to use my guides to help forge a path to the top, and how everyone could follow in behind me. Then I tried to lift the group's confidence. I preferred not to prepare or operate when surrounded by bad energy and pessimism. On K2, I sensed that the battle was being lost in the mind, but the climb was within everybody's grasp if they showed enough heart. Positivity was needed.

A lot of people might wonder why I cared so much about how confident the other climbers were feeling about their expeditions. The truth is that it would have been easy for me to behave selfishly. I could have moved over to Broad Peak, climbed there first and then returned to K2 a little later once the other parties had left the area. Instead, I wanted to show them that the impossible was within reach.

"You've already been up to Camp 4," I said. "But you only turned back because there were no fixed lines beyond that and the conditions were bad. Since then, you've had time to rest. You're strong."

"But it's so tough up there," said one climber.

"Look brother, don't talk yourself out of it. I've just climbed back-to-back mountains without sleep. In Nepal, I made rescue attempts and then climbed again the next day. You're in a much stronger position than I was on Everest, or Dhaulagiri, or Kanchenjunga. We'll lead the way and a day later, you'll summit."

I reminded them that with positive thought, courage, and discipline they would survive, but approaching K2 with a negative mindset was the fastest route to failure.

I knew the climb would still prove to be hard, regardless of my enthusiasm for adventure. In addition to the avalanches and

jawline. If just one cracked and crashed down the incline, we were done. Moving slowly around the intimidating terrain, I focused my thoughts as we advanced up the summit ridge to finally reach the peak.

It was July 24, 2019. My heart was full that morning as I braced myself against the winds, but the buzz of success was strangely fleeting. Having climbed one of the world's deadliest mountains, a climb that was steeper and riskier than the world's highest, I was reluctant to take in the clear blue skies or enjoy the moment for too long.

I wanted to get down as soon as possible for a few reasons. First, my stomach had been feeling weird for a few days, so I didn't want to linger. Second, I wanted to hit Broad Peak as quickly as possible on the next expedition. Finally, the sooner I completed the Pakistan phase, the sooner I could deal with the pressing issue of gaining the permits for Shishapangma in Tibet. There was no time for reflection.

As we moved down K2 and readied ourselves for Broad Peak, my mind felt strong. Ten peaks had been checked off the list.

CHAPTER 19

⛰

BROAD PEAK

ONCE WE FINISHED OUR CLIMB ON K2, WE RESTED AT its Base Camp for about three hours. I met up with my teammates Mingma and Halung Dorchi Sherpa, and we pressed on to Broad Peak. At 26,414 feet (8,051 m) high, it is the 12th highest mountain in the world.

I'd hoped to summit Phase Two's final mountain in one day, but more and more challenges were stacking up. We were worn out, both physically and emotionally, and I was still feeling sick. Worse, my equipment had been soaked through on K2. As we prepared at Base Camp, I made sure to air out the equipment as best I could, but there was no way of drying my heavy summit suit in such a short time.

When we started out for Camp 1, my trousers and coat felt like a wet, squishy bear hug. At a much higher altitude, that unpleasant feeling could become potentially dangerous, particularly if the moisture inside my suit turned to ice. I would literally freeze.

BROAD PEAK WAS COVERED. THERE HAD BEEN HEAVY snowfall shortly before we arrived, burying the fixed lines. A light path had been marked by some of the climbers who had made it to Camp 4 a couple of days earlier, but a lot of their footsteps had been filled in. We'd have to trailblaze our own path to the very top. As Mingma, Halung, and I charged through the snow, my body seemed unable to cope. Not only was the rope to the summit buried, requiring us to yank it up through a few feet of snow, but we were having to lift our knees high, over and over again, for any forward momentum. My breathing was labored. The energy levels I'd once carried in reserve were depleted.

Physically I seemed near failure. But realizing that a record-breaking time for finishing the Pakistan peaks was within reach, I refocused my mind. Stubbornly, I worked even harder, striding forcefully to the top, step by step. By the time we'd made it to 25,756 feet (7,850 m), the effort had finally taken its toll, and my back and legs were buckling. I felt exhausted. Slumped in the snow, my muscles and bones were flooded with extreme pain.

Whenever I coughed, the taste of blood seemed to cling to my tongue, a sign that the high altitude was impacting my body. Broad Peak had worn me down. At this point, it felt wise to outline a clear plan of action for our team. The bottom line was that the route to the top of Broad Peak was a beast. We needed to rest.

"Guys, we're all pretty tired," I said. "The conditions up here are tough, so we should rest a bit, regroup, and then work really hard to the top."

The plan was that we would climb a steep, narrow section toward the ridgeline. From there we could work our way over to the peak, hitting the very top at sunrise.

A few hours later, we were on the move again, oxygen masks strapped across our faces. At about 26,000 feet (8,000 m), my breathing felt increasingly labored, and when I checked in with Mingma and Halung, they confirmed that the effort felt more challenging than usual. Halung had trailed behind us for some time and had been unable to help with our work as we climbed.

At first, I thought our combined slump was due to having just climbed K2, but the decline in energy was a bit alarming. When I checked our oxygen cylinders, the truth about our slowing pace was revealed: *We were out of air!* We would need to traverse the 164 feet (50 m) or so to Broad Peak's summit as quickly as we could or go back to Camp 3 for more oxygen. It was one of those life-or-death decisions where evaluation and decision-making were key.

WHEN I CHECKED OUR OXYGEN CYLINDERS, THE TRUTH ABOUT OUR SLOWING PACE WAS REVEALED: *WE WERE OUT OF AIR!*

We decided to forge ahead and get the job done. We would be doing this without a visible route to follow, instead relying on our GPS to steer us onward.

We walked around the mountain's ridgeline, working toward what looked like Broad Peak's highest point. But once we arrived, another, higher point emerged through the clouds ahead. And then another. Our GPS wasn't helping, and we were exhausted.

Though the worst of the weather wasn't upon us yet, it was still bitterly cold and windy; visibility was poor, and we were shrouded in thick clouds, barely able to see in front of our faces. Considering that none of us had climbed Broad Peak before, we weren't entirely sure which way to go. Only by communicating with our radio contacts at Base Camp, in Kathmandu, and in London—all of whom were linked up to another GPS to track our location—were we able to figure out our exact position. Our contacts told us where to move.

Extreme fatigue gripped us all; we became increasingly disoriented. Our lives were very much on the line. There was every chance that one of us might take a fatal misstep or make a stupid decision. At one point, I looked down and realized that we'd been climbing for some time having forgotten to connect ourselves to a rope—a top safety priority.

Disconnected from one another, I knew that if Mingma, Halung, or I slipped, there would be no chance of stopping the fall. But if we were all linked, the combined weight and effort of the group might help to slam on the brakes. Our oversight had been a result of our extreme exhaustion. I pulled out a length of line and lashed everybody together.

While I liked to carry the bare minimum of equipment and supplies during a summit push, Mingma often traveled with one or two luxuries. During a short rest, I noticed him rummaging through his rucksack until he pulled out a packet of Korean coffee. Tearing it open, he tipped the ground beans into his mouth, gesturing that we all do the same. The powder was bitter, but a caffeine kick was soon working through our systems.

Before long, on July 26, Broad Peak's summit flag appeared in the distance. We hung around for a short time, laughing bleakly at how the mountain had nearly killed us. We then took a couple of pictures before descending. There was very little joy. I couldn't wait to get down. It felt like Broad Peak had defeated us, even though we'd reached the summit under very difficult circumstances.

> IT FELT LIKE BROAD PEAK HAD DEFEATED US, EVEN THOUGH WE'D REACHED THE SUMMIT UNDER VERY DIFFICULT CIRCUMSTANCES.

On our way down, Mingma and Halung decided to sleep at Camp 3 for a few hours. But I was eager to get home, so I kept going down, wandering into a layer of thick clouds. *Big mistake.* I was soon confused, unable to locate the fixed line that would guide me all the way to the bottom of Broad Peak. At one point, I even found myself seriously close to the edge of a sheer drop, which fell several hundred feet. I was upset about my poor judgment. *Why do you do these things?* I thought. My damp summit suit was close to freezing; I was cold and unable to focus on the terrain ahead, and what I really wanted to do was sleep. Suddenly, surrendering seemed like a viable option.

If I died here, then all of this pain would end.

It had happened again. I was overwhelmed by the effort. But I wasn't beaten. The only way to get through this was positive thinking.

Turning my mind around, I found the fuel I needed. I thought of the people who had put their faith in me, the friends I had made along the way, and most of all, I considered Suchi and my family. *They needed me to get back.* Finally, I envisioned the finish line, my ascent on Shishapangma, and the reception in Kathmandu as the world learned of my successes. The fog of despair was lifting.

Just make it happen. You can't give up here.

I needed to reconnect with the ridgeline somehow. By doing so, I could hopefully locate the fixed line, and from there I'd be able to switch into autopilot. I had to look out for a visual cue. I scanned the horizon for footfalls in the snow. There, a couple of hundred feet above me, was a barely visible path, gouged into the snow by our earlier trailblaze.

I turned around, using all of my strength to go up, then to go down again, visualizing success all the way.

CHAPTER 20

THE PEOPLE'S PROJECT

AS I WORKED MY WAY BACK FROM BROAD PEAK TO home in Nepal, the obstacles in my path seemed to grow. I needed to knock them down one by one. My most pressing issue was Shishapangma. The paperwork required to climb it was still being held back by the Chinese and Tibetan authorities. This left the mission schedule up in the air. I was reluctant to admit defeat, but it was time to consider Plan B, a fallback option that might replicate the effort required to climb a 14th peak.

Considering the scale of what was being attempted, I thought about climbing one of the other Death Zone peaks again—maybe Everest, Annapurna, or K2. In the end, I decided that if worse came to worse, I should repeat Dhaulagiri. The climb was gnarly; it had also been my first big mountain expedition. I penciled in Everest as a possible bonus mission.

So far, I had broken more world records: I'd finished the Pakistan peaks in 23 days, and climbed the world's five tallest mountains (Everest, K2, Kanchenjunga, Lhotse, and Makalu) in

70 days, which was 10 days faster than my original goal of 80 days.

My other plan for climbing Shishapangma was to find an alternative way into Tibet. If sneaking across the border via some backdoor route was doable, it might be possible to scale Shishapangma without alerting the authorities. It was an option, but the plan was loaded with risk.

In the end, I knew my best hope was to convince the Chinese and Tibetan authorities to reverse their decision. If I could apply a little pressure, there was a chance I might score a permit. I decided to approach influential people in Nepal for help.

I called friends, contacting everyone I knew who might be able to arrange a meeting with key people. To my relief, appointments were made with the minister for tourism, the tourism board, and the Nepal Mountaineering Association. I was then given permission to meet with the former prime minister of Nepal, Madhav Kumar Nepal. He had connections to the Chinese government. *This was my chance.*

When I was ushered into his office, I didn't feel intimidated. My military career had taught me about the protocols of meeting people in authority. I understood how to show respect, and knew the importance of civility. I also appreciated the value of people's time. Mr. Kumar was a busy man, and I had a limited window to convince him of the importance of my project.

I briefly summarized my motives behind the 14 expeditions, first telling Mr. Kumar about my work in enhancing the reputation of the Nepali climbing community.

"I've wanted to put them back on the map," I said.

Then I explained my attempts to raise awareness of some of the environmental issues affecting the Death Zone peaks.

"Isn't this an expedition the Nepali people can unite behind?"

Mr. Kumar nodded silently. *Was this going well, or badly?* I couldn't tell.

"I also want this to be an inspiring story for generations of people, no matter where they come from. This endeavor is for mankind. That's why I'm working so hard, every day, to push the story out. Mr. Kumar, I want to prove the power of imagination. People have laughed at me, but I'm still going strong. If I can get that Chinese permit, nothing will stop me from finishing what I've started."

Mr. Kumar was smiling now. "Nims, let me make some phone calls," he said. "I can't promise the Chinese will issue the paperwork, but I'll see what I can do."

We shook hands; I felt good. I had a hunch that if the former Nepali prime minister was going to back my cause, then the Tibetan and Chinese authorities might provide the permits. I needed all the positive PR I could get. At that time, few people outside the mountain climbing community, or my social media bubble, were paying much attention to what I'd achieved. My efforts had gotten only a little fanfare in newspapers, magazines, radio, and TV, which was frustrating.

On the other hand, the mission was still gathering momentum. My social media profile increased day by day, and more people were commenting on my photos and video clips.

I'd somehow developed a knack for gathering hundreds of thousands of followers, which was mind-blowing on a personal level, but wasn't enough to translate into huge expedition funds. Still, the messages I received were inspiring. Kids shared stories they'd written about the successful expeditions so far, and they drew pictures of my team in action. Others commented on my photos. Some promised to organize environmental awareness programs at school. One or two more donations had trickled in, too. This was good progress.

My project was becoming the people's project.

GOING INTO AUGUST 2019, I WAS PLANNING THE SCHEDULE for the three final climbs: Manaslu, Cho Oyu, and Shishapangma. I was mainly working on it alone, although Suchi helped with some administrative details. Plus, I still awaited a permit from the Chinese government. Climbing mountains was exhilarating. These preparations were exhausting.

Then, Mom got sick again.

Her condition was worsening. Throughout the mission, she had been my inspiration. I was deter-

> I WAS DETERMINED TO CLIMB ALL 14 MOUNTAINS WITH HER IN MY HEART.

mined to climb all 14 mountains with her in my heart. But I was placed in an impossible position. After climbing the mountains, I'd be free to work on other money-making projects that I hoped could bring my parents together in Kathmandu. Now time was against me; that was becoming more obvious by the week. Mom had been hospitalized again, and, according to the doctor, her chances of making it through another heart operation were slim.

"Ninety-nine percent of people who have had this procedure at her age have died," said the surgeon.

She was placed on a ventilator. Fearing the worst, I called my family to come to Nepal. At that point, my brothers were living in England; my sister, Anita, flew all the way from Australia. There was a very real chance that we might have to say goodbye to our mother.

If ever I felt like taking a chance, I remembered Mom and Dad. They needed me to care for them when my work was done. I recalled how my brothers had sent me to boarding school with their Gurkha wages. I owed my family everything. All that I'd achieved so far was for them.

Mom understood that she was my inspiration. She seemed to be hanging on to life, knowing her death would shatter my dream of completing the 14 mountains. In Hinduism, when a parent dies, the family embarks on 13 days of grieving during which they mourn alone. Emotions are expressed freely, so that those left behind can get on with their lives and heal. The energy of mourning is turned into something productive.

If Mom passed, I'd have to lock myself away, eating only once a day, and even then, I would only be allowed to eat a few vegetables. While I wasn't a religious person, Mom was. I'd have happily performed the ritual for her memory, even though it would mean closing down the last three expeditions of the year. But she was much stronger than we expected. After undergoing an invasive heart operation, she pulled through.

As I sat by Mom's bedside holding her hand, I explained my plans for the coming month.

"I have only the three mountains to climb," I said. "Let me go do this."

There was a nod and a smile. But she didn't have to say anything. I knew Mom was on my side. She always had been.

CHAPTER 21

PHASE THREE IS A GO

THERE WAS FINALLY PROGRESS.

After a full month of paperwork, I was ready to press ahead with Phase Three. First, I would climb Manaslu in Nepal, and then I would go into Tibet to climb Cho Oyu. Meanwhile, Chinese and Tibetan authorities were apparently warming to the idea of granting me a permit for Shishapangma. I was holding on to hope that I would get it.

After about a week at Manaslu Base Camp, a rumor was going around that Cho Oyu was closing down for the season earlier than expected. For some reason, the Chinese authorities decided everybody should evacuate the mountain by October 1. I checked my calendar. *Oh no!* There were only two weeks remaining in September. I had to pause my Manaslu expedition and get to Cho Oyu.

I figured it was possible to climb Cho Oyu and then return to Manaslu for the summit window. I was taking some other climbers with me to climb Manaslu. There was no way I wanted to let them down. I'd given them my word that I'd be climbing with

them. The effort would be huge, though, and I had very little
room to make any mistakes. So, accompanied by Gesman, we
packed up and traveled to Tibet. After a series of border checks,
we were allowed in for what had suddenly become a rushed
expedition.

I worked tirelessly to figure out how to make it to the top of
Cho Oyu as quickly as possible, and I learned that the line-fixing
team had reached only as high as Camp 2. We offered to chip in
with setting the ropes at the higher camps and then carried our
equipment to Camp 1, dragging our oxygen cylinders, tent, and
rope with us. Soon after, we returned to Base Camp where the
real work began.

Because of the short window in which it was possible to
climb Cho Oyu, a number of expeditions were gathering at the
mountain. Among them was my friend Mingma Sherpa. He was
planning to visit the Base Camp with several high-ranking
officials from the China Tibet Mountaineering Association
(CTMA). He was also planning to climb Cho Oyu around the
same time that we were. I guessed he might be able to help convince the CTMA to grant my permit for Shishapangma. Between
meetings about weather systems, trailblazing efforts, and work-
loads, I moved between tents, trying to find him, only to discover
that the news of his arrival had been a little off. I learned that
Mingma Sherpa hadn't yet arrived, but I left a message anyway,
hoping we could talk when he came.

It was time to get going. We went from Camp 1 to Camp 2.
From there, we scooped up a long loop of rope and trailblazed for
about 1,300 feet (400 m) in one push. *Boom! Boom! Boom!* We
kept striding forward. Gesman and I reached the top of Cho Oyu
on September 23, 2019.

HAVING TICKED CHO OYU OFF THE LIST, THERE WAS NO time to celebrate. We had to get back to Manaslu as fast as possible. Our weather window was closing, so we packed up and left. I knew that once I'd climbed Manaslu, around four days after scaling Cho Oyu, I'd have ticked off 13 of the 14 Death Zone mountains. But Shishapangma still seemed out of reach.

Could I finish what I'd started?

So many people were watching now. Many of them had initially dismissed my chances of making it this far. A lot of expert climbers had doubted that I'd even last through Pakistan. The work of the Nepali climbers alongside me had also gathered plenty of attention. The goal of helping them gain a good reputation had already been achieved.

I had three things left to do: finish Manaslu and hopefully Shishapangma, bring Mom and Dad together under the same roof once more, and get the world to pay attention to some of the damage being inflicted on the environment. With the eyes of the climbing community on me, I decided that Manaslu wasn't simply a peak to be crossed off the list, it was a platform to get my message out.

Gesman and I reached the top of Manaslu on September 27, 2019. I filmed a message to share with the world.

"Today is the twenty-seventh of September," I said, as Gesman filmed me. "Here I am on the summit of Manaslu. We're not going to talk about Project Possible, but what I am going to talk about from the summit [is the environment]. For the last decade, it's pretty obvious there has been a huge, significant change in terms of global warming. There is a huge change in the melting of the ice. The Khumbu Icefall on Everest: Every day the glacier is melting—it's getting thinner and smaller and smaller. The Earth is our home. We should be more serious about it—more cautious, more focused about how we look after our planet. At the end of the day, if this one doesn't exist, we don't exist."

I didn't think about my speech in advance. The words came from the heart. They were a true reflection of what I felt for the world. As far as I was concerned, the biggest challenge faced by humankind in the coming decade or two had to be climate change, but fixing it required each of us to make major changes. If I learned anything on this journey it was that the actions of an individual had the potential to overcome the most insurmountable problems.

If I could climb the Death Zone mountains in seven months, then what was to stop another individual from finding and conquering their goals in the fields of environmental science, alternative energy, or climate action? My efforts had proved that everyone had the potential to go way beyond what was considered possible. My journey was meant to provide a glimmer of hope, a show of positive action. I wanted others to use it as inspiration for their own challenges and goals. If my work created a spark for change, however small, I'd be happy.

SOON AFTER CLIMBING MANASLU, I GOT MY PERMIT FOR Shishapangma.

How it happened is a dizzying blur of phone calls, emails, and meetings. But in the end, it took just one person to tip the balance in my favor: Mingma Sherpa. The man I'd so nearly met with at Cho Oyu's Base Camp had learned of my efforts and was impressed by my commitment to do whatever I could to get to the final peak.

The news of my approved permit first filtered back to me after returning to Manaslu's Base Camp. I was hopeful, but I needed to see it for myself before I let myself get too excited.

I didn't have to wait long. The Chinese and Tibetan authorities got in touch with me. They wanted to talk, and the conversation was positive. Having taken into account the scale of my project, they decided to open up Shishapangma for a brief time so I could finish the mission. I was so relieved. After all the stress, the finish line was in sight.

AFTER ALL THE STRESS, THE FINISH LINE WAS IN SIGHT.

However, there was a catch. Mingma Sherpa explained that in order to access the mountain, he would have to travel with me to Base Camp. It was a condition set by the CTMA. At first, I was unsure. I worried it might be an attempt to get in on my hard work, or perhaps a way for the CTMA to grab some attention for themselves. In the end, I put aside my concerns and remembered the potentially positive impact of a successful mission.

If Mingma Sherpa coming with us to Base Camp meant the difference between completing the 14th mountain or missing out on my end goal, then I was happy to have an extra person in the camp. He would, at the very least, provide additional manpower for the team. Mingma Sherpa quickly proved himself an asset. He acted as an expedition resource and a fixer for some of the more complicated parts of the project involving the authorities.

As we checked the weather and figured out the best date to climb, we received a warning from a member of the mountain's management office.

"The mountain is too dangerous," he said. "The weather is so bad."

He was right. The snow was coming down hard, but I'd climbed in worse conditions. I tried to tell him that I could take on the risk. I was used to it and knew what to do.

The liaison manager shook his head. "Sorry, but no," he said. "If anything happens to you, it will be my responsibility. And there's an avalanche problem."

In the end, I gave it my all to convince him to let us go. I explained how I'd fixed the lines at K2 when nobody else had been willing to climb. There was a mention of my efforts for the G200E in 2017, when the entire project had hung in the balance. And I mentioned I had conducted 19 successful 26,000-feet (8,000-m) expeditions in total, 13 in 2019. Nobody had died on the mountain under my leadership.

As I explained my position, it felt hard to keep my frustrations under control, but I knew that I had to keep my composure. Eventually, the liaison officer backed down. On the eve of the summit push, I sat at the foot of Shishapangma and gathered my thoughts.

Nims, take it easy, I said to myself. *You are here now; you only have to stay alive. Don't take any unnecessary risks. Control everything. Stay calm. Stay cool. The mission isn't done unless you come back home alive.*

I looked to Shishapangma's peak. Clouds had swept in; an ominous rumble of thunder was echoing through the valley below. As I watched, it was impossible not to be in awe of the size and scale of what lay ahead.

There was a rush of inspiration. If I could channel the mountain's spirit and become protected from pain, stress, and fear, then nothing could stop me. Before I rested for the night, I asked Shishapangma some final questions.

Okay, will you let me do this?

Can I? Or can I not?

THE WEATHER ON THE WAY UP WAS HORRIFIC. IT WAS AS IF the mountain wanted to deny me the final climb, or at least find out if I was truly worthy of finishing the job. Winds of 56 miles an hour (90 km/h) blasted Mingma David, Geljen, and me. We trudged up the mountain through the lower camps, fixing the lines and anchors along the way. Nothing could hold me back, though an avalanche came close. We had been working our way to Camp 1, and for a few moments, as the team rested, I took the drone from my backpack. Climbing Shishapangma was a big deal. And it was the end of my mission, which was emotional. I hoped to capture as much of the final expedition on film as possible. When the winds settled down a little, I sent the drone into the air, filming the team as they stepped up the mountain.

The ground started to tremble. I was probably around five or 10 minutes behind the others, and when I looked up, I saw a slab of snow had cracked below their position on the line. Slowly it was shearing away from the mountain. I didn't know what had triggered the avalanche, but as it jolted and began its fall down Shishapangma's side, I became an accidental passenger. I was surfing the snow, and there was no point in fighting its power.

As I glided down the slope, the ground was breaking up around me. In an instant, the snow swallowed my body whole and then spit me out. As I prepared to be pulled under for good, the world came to a standstill. I looked down. The avalanche was billowing away below me, breaking up on rocks and puffing up a white cloud. The snow I'd been standing on had somehow come to a stop. My life was spared.

I can't believe it, brother, I laughed to myself. *You've come all this way and nearly died on the last expedition.*

The drone stayed in the bag from then on.

As I worked my way back to the line where Mingma and Geljen were waiting, I felt surprised that the emotional aftershock of yet another near-death experience was not affecting me. I had been through and survived a lot already. My crampons seemed fused to my body; my ice axe was an extra limb. I felt good.

For the push to Shishapangma's summit, we took a new line to the top. As we moved past Camp 2 the weather calmed. Clouds cleared around us, the winds seemed to die away, and everything became peaceful. I was calm, too. The last half of the climb on Shishapangma turned into a slow and steady trek. The climb was straightforward, but emotionally the effort felt heavy as I stepped to the peak on October 29.

It was done.

Everything I had achieved up until that moment started to dawn on me. I'd silenced the doubters by climbing the 14 highest mountains in the world in six months and six days. I'd shown what was achievable with imagination and a determined spirit, and I helped to shine

> EVERYTHING I HAD ACHIEVED UP UNTIL THAT MOMENT STARTED TO DAWN ON ME.

a light on some of the challenges being faced by our planet and its people.

I'd made the impossible possible.

In the distance I could see Everest, the place where it all began, and the feelings I'd bottled up for so long rushed at me at once: pride, happiness, and love. I thought of Suchi and my friends and family. Most of all I thought of Mom and Dad. Tears rolled down my cheeks.

In a way, the mission had been a process of personal discovery. By climbing the 14 peaks, I figured out who I was. I wanted to know how far I could push myself.

I'm not sure where that desire actually came from, but it was apparent from an early age. As a small boy in Chitwan, I'd turn over rocks for hours at a time in a stream, in search of crabs and prawns, and I wouldn't quit until I'd peeked under every single one. Fast-forward 30 years and nothing much had changed. My spirit was still the same; only the situation had evolved. Rather than exploring the local river, I was climbing across the Death Zone. With that achievement almost complete, I was already starting to imagine beyond it.

I wanted more. *But where could I go next?*

Standing on the peak of Shishapangma, I took in the view, feeling the bitter cold on my face. Then I called home and told Mom what I'd achieved, and where I planned to go next.

"I've done it!" I shouted into the phone. "And I'm okay."

The line was crackling, but I could just make out her laughter.

"Get home safe, son," she said. "I love you."

AT THE PEAK

THE ENORMITY OF WHAT I'D ACCOMPLISHED DIDN'T hit me for days. The following morning, I traveled back across the border to Nepal where a hero's welcome was awaiting our team—the Special Forces of high-altitude mountaineering. Word had spread about my record-breaking achievements. Not only had I managed to climb the world's 14 highest peaks, shattering the world record by more than seven years, but I'd also posted the fastest time for climbing from the summit of Everest to Lhotse and then to Makalu. The Pakistan peaks had been nailed in 23 days, and I'd climbed the five highest mountains, Everest, K2, Kanchenjunga, Lhotse, and Makalu, in 70 days, 10 days fewer than my original goal of 80. Additionally, I'd climbed the most 26,000-foot (8,000-m) peaks in a single season (spring) by topping Annapurna, Dhaulagiri, Kanchenjunga, Everest, Lhotse, and Makalu in 31 days. The mission was an overwhelming success. I called up Mom again. A party was being arranged in Kathmandu and despite her condition, the doctors assured me that she was well enough to travel. I suggested she join me for a celebratory helicopter ride. At first, she wasn't sure. I told her how important she was to me, and how the mission had been the biggest achievement of my life.

"I want you to be a part of it," I said.

"Yes, I want to come," she said, eventually.

When we arrived at the Kathmandu Tribhuvan Airport, the scene was incredible. A marching band was playing, dozens of photographers and journalists had arrived, and a huge crowd circled the airport. I couldn't quite get my head around it. Until that point, I think Mom had considered my climbing a crazy hobby, a risky project that filled me with joy. Not for one minute did she realize that my work was being followed by the world, not on a scale this big anyway. Seeing the crowds and the fanfare surrounding my successes, she understood.

As the rotary blades on the chopper slowed above us, a white Range Rover pulled around with the flags of Great Britain and Nepal fixed on top. The British ambassador to Nepal, Richard Morris, stepped out, and once we'd shaken hands, he thanked me for my efforts.

"We're so proud of you," he said. "What you've achieved is unbelievable."

When we were eventually driven through the city to a reception, the crowds followed us everywhere.

In the months after the 14 mountains had been completed, I did everything in my power to bring Mom and Dad together in a new home. I secured a loan with a bank in Nepal, and I borrowed money from my family. I was also earning money guiding expeditions and doing motivational speaking. With the money I earned, I found a nice house in Kathmandu that would work for both my parents.

Excited about them moving in, we completed the paperwork in early 2020 and started moving Dad out of the old house in Chitwan. On February 25, 2020, Suchi and I flew to Nepal to bring them together, but when we landed, the phone rang. *We were too late.* Mom had passed away a couple hours earlier. My heart was broken. Everything I had achieved was inspired by her spirit.

I spent the next 13 days taking part in the Hindu mourning period. During this time of quiet, I was able to reflect on my mother's life. At the end of the 13 days, I decided to turn my grief into a powerful, positive energy. Because of the love and support of my family, I'd been able to push myself to the absolute limit, proving to the world that anything was possible.

It was great to know that the reputation of the Nepalese Sherpa guides had also been amplified. The guys I'd climbed with were being placed on a pedestal. They had come to be regarded as some of the world's best climbers, and rightly so. We worked as a relatively small expedition unit, in teams of three, four, or five, but we moved with the power of 10 bulls and the heart of a hundred men. They deserved it all.

As for my next move, all I know is that I want to be at the world's highest point again, because for me that is the only way to live.

LESSONS FROM THE DEATH ZONE

1. Leadership isn't always about what *you* want.

Having made it to Base Camp at Dhaulagiri during Phase One of the mission, it was obvious that some of the guys in my team were struggling, physically and mentally. As the team leader, I had to motivate them.

It's easy to work at your own pace in a group setting, especially if you're the fastest or strongest in the pack, but the people around you will soon lose faith. It's important to show that you're a team player, to put yourself in others' shoes. In this case, I took the team aside for a little rest and recovery to bring them back mentally and physically. We had to work through some terrible conditions a few days later as a consequence of our slight delay, but that one action told the team that the mission wasn't only about me—it was about all of us.

As a result, they broke their backs to work for the cause over the next six months.

2. The little things count most on the big mountains.

Over the years, I've developed techniques for lightening my workload when climbing the big mountains. One of the most important involves my breathing. Whenever I'm at high altitude, I wear a buff—a garment that covers the neck and lower part of the face. It protects my face from the sun and the biting cold, but it's hard to wear one without fogging up my goggles or sunglasses with the condensation from my breath.

To fix that, I changed the way I inhale and exhale. Pursing my lips, I take air in through my nose and then blow down, away from the goggles. The cold air comes in through the buff, warming it slightly. This protects my lungs from failing in the subzero temperatures. It might sound like a minor detail, but it's a technique that saves my body from hypothermia because the air I'm breathing in is not as cold. It also protects my fingers from frostbite because I don't have to take off my gloves to get a cloth to clean my goggles. (All of which is exhausting to do at high altitude.)

Taking care of the little things feeds into the bigger goal. For you, that might mean knowing the specific details of a game so you can succeed at it, or learning what shoes are best for preventing blisters for a sport you play. They may be details, but they can make all the difference.

3. Never underestimate the challenge ahead.

I first learned about the dangers associated with underestimating a climb in 2015. As an intermediate mountaineer, I climbed Mount Aconcagua in the Andes mountain range in Argentina. The mountain is one of the Seven Summits, a peak with a serious reputation, and at 22,838 feet (6,961 m), it's a challenging test of high altitude.

Mountaineers with ambitions of climbing in the Death Zone often use Aconcagua as an early test of their abilities. For this climb, rope skills are not needed to get to the summit. A lot of people figure it's a fairly easy mountain to climb. That was my attitude anyway.

Having flicked through a few climbing guides and magazines, and having looked at a ton of photographs featuring kids and old couples climbing to Aconcagua's peak, I was dismissive. Friends I'd made during my expeditions to Dhaulagiri and Lobuche East figured Aconcagua would be a breeze for me.

"You'll smash it," said one. "Trek to Base Camp in a day. Then take a day or two to summit and head back. No dramas."

I was so convinced of my ability, and Aconcagua's apparently gentle temperament, that I didn't bother packing a summit suit for my expedition. I was traveling during the summer months at the start of the year when the weather is pretty warm in the Southern Hemisphere. I also packed hiking pants, a waterproof coat, and a pair of mountain boots. But once I entered the national park where Aconcagua is located, it started to snow.

Aconcagua is a remote mountain; it took a trek of 11 hours to reach Base Camp. I was traveling solo and had to use my map and compass to get there because the paths normally marking the route up were now smothered by heavy snowdrifts. When I arrived at Base Camp and checked in with the other climbers, the mood was gloomy. A number of people had made a push for the summit but had been turned around by the weather.

"It's so dangerous up there," said a friend from the International Federation of Mountain Guides Associations. "The avalanche risk is high and the weather is seriously cold."

I figured I knew better. I borrowed boots from another climber, a pair far sturdier than the ones I'd brought. I also borrowed a down jacket. Then, I pushed to the top, the weather closing in tightly around me. What should have been a fairly straightforward trek became as grueling as my first ever climb on a Death Zone peak. When I made it to 980 feet (300 m) from the peak, I came close to giving up.

I climbed without oxygen, and altitude sickness was kicking in. I felt close to passing out. My vision also blurred. All my hopes of becoming an elite climber seemed to hang in the balance. *Nims, if you can't make it to the top here, how can you expect to take on Everest?* I was shaken.

I took a sip of water and opened up a chocolate bar.

You have the speed to climb super quickly. Use it.

Pushing on to the summit, I couldn't wait to turn around. I had learned two important lessons: Never underestimate the mountain you're about to climb, no matter how easy other people think it may be. And be confident, but always show respect.

From then on, I did my due diligence on every expedition. I readied myself for the challenges ahead and told myself that any mountain had the potential to be my last if I didn't handle it with care. I got a serious reminder when I didn't follow this rule: I made the mistake of underestimating Gasherbrum I during Phase Two of the mission, and it kicked me hard.

Whatever you're doing, treat your challenge with respect. You won't be likely to suffer any unexpected surprises that way.

4. Hard work is everything.

You're not going to achieve your dream by just fantasizing about it. You must dedicate yourself to it entirely and put in the time to work hard for it. That will give you the best chance of making your dream come true.

As a kid, I got so angry when I was beaten in a race by a runner from another school that I started getting up in the middle of the night to train in secret. I took that same attitude when training to become a Gurkha. If we were required to run 19 miles (30 km) in training, I'd tack on another 12 miles (20 km) to push myself. I knew I wanted to make it into the Special Forces. The job had become everything, and I invested all my efforts in it.

Rather than thinking, hoping, and waiting for your next project or challenge, take action and go for it.

5. A person's true nature shows up in life-or-death situations.

At Base Camp, when the weather is sunny and warm, climbers take selfies and mess around and talk about how they're going to conquer the mountain. Once the bad weather whips in, and it becomes important to stay focused and disciplined, climbers' true personalities emerge. They can act selfishly, their work slacks off, and they sometimes disregard the safety of others. When you're climbing a mountain, everyone's attitude and effort matter because they affect everyone. It's easy to act like you know it all, but your words and actions in times of hardship are what prove who you really are. You learn a lot about someone when things get tough.

6. Turn a nightmare situation into something positive.

During my first climbs of Everest, Lhotse, and Makalu, my oxygen was stolen on the mountain. I'd asked for cylinders to be left at a number of camps, but when I arrived at each one, it became apparent that they had been swiped. At first, I was furious, an understandable reaction given the circumstances, but it was important to stay calm. Losing my temper would cause me to waste energy, which, on a mountain, can be hazardous. As I explained in Lesson 2, the little things count the most on big mountains. A negative response, an emotional rant, could cost me dearly later.

I calmed down and practiced positive thinking.

Maybe someone had severe altitude sickness and needed my cylinders to save themselves, I told myself. *In which case, fair enough.* Even though it might not have been true, it was a vital self-defense mechanism. If I'd sulked and moaned about my missing air, I would have wasted my own energy, when I should have been concentrating on the mission ahead.

Thinking positively is the only way to survive at more than 26,000 feet (8,000 m).

7. Give 100 percent to the present ... because it's all you've got.

There were moments during the selection process in the military when a program of grueling work was laid out ahead of me: weeks of drills, marches, and exercises in unpleasant conditions. I'd have to push myself to a breaking point. It would have been easy to feel overwhelmed by the intimidating workload, or stressed that the first day's 30-mile (48-km) run might burn me out for an even longer run the next day. Instead, I gave everything to the job at hand and kept my sights on the present moment. Doing so allowed me to get rid of any doubts, helping me handle an intimidating challenge.

I applied the same attitude to my mission to climb the 14 Death Zone peaks. While working across a mountain, I tried my best not to think about the next expedition because I knew I might not make it if I took my eye off the mountain I was on. To be focused on Broad Peak while scaling K2 could cause me to lose focus. I had to give that day my all, because I knew the consequences if I didn't.

Tomorrow might not happen.

8. Never lie. Never make excuses.

There were times when I could have cut corners on the mountain. Following the G200E in 2017, when my friend Nishal offered me a helicopter ride from Namche Bazaar to Makalu's Camp 2 and not to Base Camp, I turned him down. His help would have made it easier for me to become the first person to climb Everest twice and Lhotse and Makalu in a single climbing season. But it wouldn't have been done properly. Sure, nobody on the planet would have known apart from Nishal. But I'd have to live with that knowledge for the rest of my life.

It's easy to make excuses or to take the easy way out. By lying to yourself, though, you're asking to fail. Lying or making excuses for sloppy actions or a lack of hard work, or anything else, means you've broken a promise to yourself. Once you do that, you'll screw up over and over again.

For example, it would have been quite easy for me to give up on K2. I wouldn't have been the first to do so. Had I abandoned the project because of a lack of funding, nobody would have blamed me. But there was no way I was going to let myself off the hook, no matter how easy it might have been.

If I say that I'm going to run for an hour, I'll run for a full hour. If I plan to do 300 pushups in a training session, I won't quit until I've done them all. Brushing off the effort would only be letting myself down. I don't want that for myself and neither should you. We all have what it takes to reach our goals.

THE WORLD RECORDS

 Fastest time to climb all 14 mountains that are higher than 26,000 feet (8,000 m):
Six months, six days

 Fastest time from the summit of Everest to the summit of Lhotse and the summit of Makalu:
48 hours, 30 minutes

 Fastest time to climb the top five highest mountains in the world (Kanchenjunga, Everest, Lhotse, Makalu, and K2):
70 days

 Fastest time to climb all five mountains that are higher than 26,000 feet (8,000 m) in Pakistan (K2, Nanga Parbat, Broad Peak, Gasherbrum I, and Gasherbrum II):
23 days

 Most 26,000-feet (8,000-m) peaks summited during a single season (spring): Six (Annapurna, Dhaulagiri, Kanchenjunga, Everest, Lhotse, and Makalu)
31 days

ACKNOWLEDGMENTS

WHEN WRITING A BOOK OF THIS KIND, IT'S HARD to remember all the people who helped me to make Project Possible a reality, so I'll do my best here. Hopefully, I won't leave anybody out.

Without the support of my expedition sponsors, Project Possible would never have happened. At the top of the thank-you list stands Bremont, which has made a series of Project Possible watches and helped me overcome the financial hurdles that threatened to stop my dream from becoming a reality. A salute also goes out to Silxo, Osprey, Ant Middleton, Digi2aL, Hama Steel, Summit Oxygen, OMNIRISC, The Royal Hotel, Intergage, AD Construction Group, Branding Science, AMTC Group, Everence, ThruDark, Kenya Airways, KGH Group, Kathmandu Marriott Hotel, and Premier Insurance.

Logistical support for the mission was provided by Elite Himalayan Adventures, Seven Summit Treks, and Climbalaya. Although the majority of filming above base camp was done by me and my team, some assistance for the forthcoming film of my story arrived courtesy of Sagar Gurung, Alit Gurung, and Sandro Gromen-Hayes, who also joined me at K2 Base Camp and climbed with me on Manaslu. I'd also like to thank everyone working hard to put the hours of footage together at Noah Media Group, especially Torquil Jones and Barry Smith, and thanks also to Mark Webber for the introduction. Help on the mission also arrived from the Special Boat Service Association (SBSA) and Ambassador Durga Subedi and so many key figures from Nepal: the Nepal Government; the Nepal Mountaineering Association; the Nepal Tourism Department; Kedar Bahadur Adhikari, the former secretary from the Ministry of Culture, Tourism, and Civil Aviation; Madhav Kumar Nepal, the former prime minister of Nepal; Ishwar Pokhrel, the former deputy defense minister of Nepal; Inspector General of Police Shailendra Khanal; and Sonam Sherpa of Yeti Group. A big thanks also has to go to Brigadier Dan Reeves for all his help.

In the U.K., an administration team helped me to figure out a way of managing my PR and all the other logistical issues that kick in while climbing to the top of an 8,000er. Most of all this includes my supportive wife, Suchi, plus Project Possible's helpers: Wendy Faux, Steve and Tiffany Curran, Luke Hill, and Kishore Rana. Thanks also to all the clients who joined me on my adventure: Hakon Asvang and Rupert Jones-Warner (Annapurna); Stefi Troguet (Nanga Parbat); and Steve Davis, Amy McCulloch, Glenn McCrory, Deeya Pun, and Stefi Troguet (Manaslu); plus everyone from all over the world who donated to the mission on GoFundMe and supported the project by picking up merchandise. There were many organizations that helped me along the way, and I'm extremely appreciative of all of them, but my gratitude goes out to the Nepali climbing community, my Sherpa brothers, and the Gurkha and Nepalese communities: Myagdi Organisation UK, Madat Shamuha, Magar Association UK, Friendly Brothers Dana Serophero Community UK, Pun Magar

ACKNOWLEDGMENTS

Samaj UK, Pun Magar Society UK, Pelkachour and Chhimeki Gaule Samaj UK, Tamu Pye Lhu Sangh UK, and the Maidstone Gurkha Nepalese Community.

My team from the 2017 world-record-breaking climbs of Everest, Lhotse, and Makalu also deserve my gratitude: Lakpa Sherpa, Jangbu Sherpa, Halung Dorchi Sherpa, and Mingma Dorchi Sherpa.

Without my family, none of this would have been possible. Mum and Dad indulged my adventurous spirit as a kid and allowed me to follow my heart to the mountains after I'd promised to bring them together under one roof. My brothers, Kamal, Jit, and Ganga, and my sister, Anita, encouraged me to follow the noble life into the Gurkhas. And there's a long list of friends, to name check, in and out of the military: Staz, Louis, Paul Daubner, Gaz Banford, Lewis Phillips, CP Limbu, Chris Sylvan, Dawa Sherpa, Ramesh Silwal, Khadka Gurung, Subash Rai, Govinda Rana, Thaneswar Gurangai, Peter Cunningham, Shrinkhala Khatiwada, Dan, Bijay Limbu, Mira Acharya, Stuart Higgins, Phil Macey, Rupert Swallow, Al Mack, Greg Williams, Mingma Sherpa, Danny Rai, Dhan Chand, Shep, Tashi Sherpa, Sobhit Gauchan, Shiva Bahadur Sapkota, and Gulam.

Finally, this book wouldn't have happened without the hard work of everyone at Hodder & Stoughton, especially Rupert Lancaster, Cameron Myers, Caitriona Horne, and Rebecca Mundy. Thanks to my agents at The Blair Partnership, Neil Blair and Rory Scarfe. Finally, I would like to thank my friend and brother Matt Allen for putting his heart and mind into capturing my story. Without his help (from his heart) this book wouldn't have been possible.

—Nirmal Purja, 2022

PHOTO CREDITS